Rolling Thunder

ROLLING THUNDER
Understanding Policy and Program Failure

JAMES CLAY THOMPSON

The University of North Carolina Press
Chapel Hill

© 1980 The University of North Carolina Press
All rights reserved
Manufactured in the United States of America
Library of Congress Catalog Card Number 79-11768
Cloth edition, ISBN 0-8078-1390-7
Paper edition, ISBN 0-8078-1391-5

Library of Congress Cataloging in Publication Data

Thompson, James Clay, 1943–
  Rolling Thunder.

  Bibliography: p.
  Includes index.
  1. Vietnamese Conflict, 1961–1975 — United States.
2. Vietnamese Conflict, 1961–1975 — Aerial operations,
American. 3. United States — Politics and government —
1961–1963. 4. United States — Politics and government —
1963–1969. I. Title.
DS558.T47   959.704'33'73   79-11768
ISBN 0-8078-1390-7
ISBN 0-8078-1391-5 pbk.

For my mother and father

    . . . they gave so much

For my son, Jim

    . . . who, I hope, will never see the ordeal of war

Contents

Illustrations

Illustrations

Tables, Figures, and Maps

Tables

Figures

Maps

Preface

This study had its origins while I was an employee of the Department of Defense. When I joined the department in 1965 as an intelligence analyst, the war in Vietnam was escalating rapidly. Bombing operations against North Vietnam had begun in the spring of that year, and in July—the very week I came "on board"—President Lyndon Johnson announced the commitment of an additional hundred thousand ground troops to Vietnam. Shortly afterward, United States Marines began pouring ashore at Da Nang. From 1965 to 1969, I watched the war from the inside, as my job placed me at a crossroads of information flowing in from the field and among agencies, bureaus, and departments in Washington. Since the perspective that is offered here is from Washington looking out at the conflict in Asia, I do not deal with the strategy or tactics in the field. Rather, I focus on the organizations in Washington as they processed information, evaluated operations, issued weekly (monthly and quarterly) reports, and so on. The central themes of the study are two: that senior United States leaders failed to understand the organizations of which they thought they were in charge and that there was a failure in strategic thinking about the impact of air power on a revolutionary war situation. That policymakers also appear to have misunderstood the global strategic capabilities and the role of the United States is also of interest, but not central to this work. It is amazing that policymakers really believed that if the United States failed to crush the revolution in South Vietnam (where only about 2 percent of the population of Asia lives), the whole global international system that has been dominated by the United States since 1945 would come unraveled and the world's foremost power would be reduced to a "pitiful, helpless giant." Such simpleminded thinking would not survive even an introductory course in world politics, but it was widely believed at that time by powerful men, who made others pay with their lives and fortunes for it.

When I joined the Defense Department, I believed, as did most Americans in 1964–65, that what we were doing in Vietnam was proper. Not until I "got inside" and gained access to the classified documents on the conflict did my views of the effort change. And, as my own doubts grew, it became apparent that numerous others within the government shared those misgivings. In the early days, such doubts were only whispered among a few. As the conflict grew into full-fledged war, opponents of the bombing within the government increasingly began to make their views known. If the war in the field was characterized by artillery, bombs, mines, gunfire, and napalm, the war in the bureaucracy was marked by meetings with endless disagreements among individuals representing various agencies, by memoranda circulated for comments, by telephone conversations (on- and off-the-record), and by "back-channel" communications (of which there is no record) to units in the field. I vividly remember one meeting in which there was a dispute between personnel from different agencies over the placement of a prepositional phrase in an intelligence summary. The argument lasted about three hours.

Probably my greatest single shock upon entering the government was my discovery that decisions were not made in the manner I had been taught they were made. I had learned that decisions were made in quiet meetings in which policymakers considered alternatives, weighed options, and estimated consequences. What I saw was confusion, misunderstandings, foulups, time deadlines so tight that sufficient information could not be gathered, and occasional loss of tempers. Once, when I had accidentally been given a bit of information I was not supposed to have, one official turned purple in the face and shouted, "Who gave that to you? I am going to get that bastard!" He paid no attention to my analysis.

An author always benefits from the comments and advice of many kind and considerate individuals. My experience with this book has not been any different. While I was at the University of Michigan, Thomas Anton, Basil Georgopolous, Harold Jacobson, A. F. K. Organski, and Allen S. Whiting helped guide this study in many ways. Harry Howe Ransom of Vanderbilt University also offered wise counsel. Andrew Scott of The University of North Carolina at Chapel Hill made many valuable suggestions. My colleagues at The University of North Carolina at Greensboro have also been supportive. I must also thank Richard Vidmer, formerly of the University of Virginia, now with the Office of Congressman Don Bailey, and Dan Coughenour of Ann Arbor, for their help and valuable advice. And to Linda Palsgaard and Maggie Davis go special thanks—they helped to transform sometimes unreadable scribbles into a completed manuscript. I would also like to thank Ron Maner for providing the index. Finally, the editors at The University of North Carolina Press, Malcolm Call, Sandra Eisdorfer, and Jan McInroy, have been extremely helpful. All of the errors that remain are, of course, my own.

Rolling Thunder

O Lord my God! When I in awesome wonder
Consider all the worlds* Thy hands have made
I see the stars, I hear the rolling* thunder

From the hymn, "How Great Thou Art"
by Stuart K. Hine

1. Introduction

In January 1968, during the Vietnamese holiday known as Tet, the North Vietnamese and Viet Cong military forces in South Vietnam launched a military offensive throughout South Vietnam. Capturing Hue, the old imperial capital of all of Vietnam, and several other South Vietnamese cities, the attackers also launched a daring guerrilla attack on the American embassy and many of its personnel. In the two weeks that the offensive lasted, hundreds of American soldiers were killed and wounded. Although the Tet offensive was eventually blunted and thousands of the attackers killed, the sight of guerrillas inside the compound of the American embassy, recorded by television cameras and shown during the evening news on the major American networks, shocked the American public. Only a few weeks before the Tet offensive, the American military commander in Vietnam, General William C. Westmoreland, had flown to Washington to tell the National Press Club (and the American people) that the enemy was being defeated, that American soldiers would soon be coming home, that "we have reached the point where the end begins to come into view."[1]

The Tet offensive is a seminal event in the history of American foreign policy. It marks the high-water point of the flood of American power that arose after World War II ended. Following the Tet offensive, the policy of expanding American involvement in Indochina was reversed and the American withdrawal from Indochina began. Seven years later, the last few Americans (of a number that at one time included 565,000 combat troops) departed from Saigon as resistance to the Communist forces collapsed.

Although numerous accounts of American involvement in Vietnam have been written, the explanations of what Bernard Brodie has called "a story of virtually unmitigated disasters that we have inflicted on ourselves and even more on others" are not conclusive.[2] Even the central questions of how the United States became involved and why American forces remained so long have eluded adequate answers.[3]

The debate over these questions has tended to focus on personalities and their view of the world. Would the United States have remained in Vietnam had President John F. Kennedy not been murdered? Was the war the fault of the best and the brightest of American decision makers who had been seduced by the old sin of hubris?[4] Other students of American foreign policy have argued that America continued its involvement because of a fear of American presidents that the loss of another country to communism would cause a domestic political reaction,[5] because of requirements for raw materials for American industry and of concerns over the economic impact of the loss of the Indochina market,[6] or because of a kind of intoxication with power and a concomitant lack of moral concern for policy results.[7] Still other analysts have suggested that combinations of these factors were at work or that senior American officials shared a widespread misperception that the turmoil in Indochina was part of communism's worldwide expansionist effort.[8]

The examination of American foreign policy set forth in this volume proceeds from the assumption that such questioning fails to provide satisfying answers because it ignores the impact of organizational processes and politics upon foreign policy. It is the contention of this study that such arguments lead to a misunderstanding of the foreign policy process. The agony of American involvement persisted because of the nature of the organizations within the United States government that dealt with questions of foreign policy. Organizational processes, for example, tended to block certain intelligence information indicating that American programs were working poorly. Organizational politics frequently influenced processes of decision making to such a degree that major disagreements were muted by a process of compromising the contradictory views into the lowest common denominator of agreement, thus making it difficult for leaders to discover that the unanimous recommendation was unanimous only because it was so general.

This contention raises further fundamental questions, along the line of "Who's in charge here?" Traditionally, analysts have viewed foreign policy as the result of decisions made by the president and his senior aides. Lengthy and sometimes emotional descriptions have been presented of a lonely president making painful decisions.[9] Thus whether American policy in Indochina was the result of a fear of a domestic political uproar, an intoxication with power, a misperception of the sources of the turmoil in Indochina, a desire to protect known or potential economic investments and markets, or a combination of these factors, the arguments most commonly offered to explain that policy share the notion, albeit in varying degrees, that major policy actions have important causes, that governmental leaders choose as they do for important reasons. Although each of the cited arguments suggests different important reasons, all are similar in that they assume that leaders "make" foreign policy and that they choose and act on the basis of attempts to minimize perceived "costs" and maximize perceived "gains." Policy is deduced by explaining what costs leaders are trying to avoid and what gains they are trying to achieve. When disagreements arise between analysts defending or attacking a particular president, for example, the dispute usually hinges on the notion that one president would not have paid the costs or tried to attain the gains that another president did. Central to all of the commonly offered explanations are, then, the ideas of goals, costs, and gains as perceived by leaders.

This idea of overarching goals and clearly perceived costs and gains has recently come under attack from several fronts. One direction of criticism has been that of social psychology. In a cogent study of the effects of group dynamics on national security decision making, Irving Janis suggests that characteristics of small-group decision making may be central to explanation of foreign policy decisions. Janis identifies eight main effects of small groups on the process of making decisions and suggests that the most crucial variable is "group cohesiveness." When individual members of a group attempt to maintain the warmth and friendliness that characterize cohesiveness, they make poor decisions. The thrust of Janis's findings is that it is possible that policy decisions may be made on the basis of values other than overarching "national interest."[10]

Criticism has also come from some students of the presidency. George Reedy, one of President Lyndon Johnson's press secretaries, has pictured Johnson as isolated from the harsh realities of the world by an overprotective staff. Such isolation may result in presidential decisions being made with an inadequate understanding of events.[11]

From the perspective of organization theory, other analysts have attacked the notion that major decisions—dispatching of troops, breaking diplomatic relations, and the like—are made only after careful examination of alternatives and consequences. After studying the impact of organizational structure, processes, and politics upon decision making, some analysts have concluded that major events may be the culmination of a series of seemingly inconsequential decisions that, over time, snowball into actions of great importance. Major events, according to some students of organizations, may have minor causes.[12]

These criticisms raise disturbing questions. How and to what extent are leaders constrained by their staffs and the bureaucracies that they, in theory, direct? What are the effects of the situational setting in which decisions are made? To what extent is policy the result of a complex interplay between the leadership and the permanent bureaucracies?

Most studies have rested on the assumption that leadership determines policy and members of permanent government bureaucracies—the career civil servants and military professionals—then follow the dictates of the leaders. This assumption is fundamental to the theory of democratic government: that changing a small group of high-level officials will ultimately change the actions of the mass of employees. The compliance of subordinates is crucial to democratic government. But what if the subordinate members of the bureaucracy exert enough influence to change the policy of the elected officials? What if there is extensive subordinate noncompliance with the dictates of leadership? The challenge to democratic theory seems profound and fundamental.

According to Morton Halperin, there in fact *is* extensive subordinate noncompliance in the arena of foreign policy decision making. Noncompliance, Halperin suggests, may be a result of subordinates' not knowing what leaders want, of their inability to do what leaders want, or of their refusal to do what leaders want.[13] Thus, policy execution may be strongly affected by the willingness (or unwillingness) of career officials to carry out the decisions handed down by their superiors. Few studies of the effects of organizational structure and behavior have centered on the execution of policy decisions; most have focused instead on the internal infighting prior to the decision.

That career officials fail to implement the decisions made by leaders highlights a critical aspect of the policy process. Once policy has been decided and programs are being implemented, how does leadership determine the effects of those programs? To accomplish this, programs must be monitored. Feedback mechanisms are therefore crucial. In the study of policy change, both the type of feedback (i.e., what kinds of indicators are used to measure program effects) and the means of processing the feedback (i.e., what organizations collect information and through what channels does the information flow) are important. The study of feedback should help to answer how and at what point leadership decides to re-examine policy or to alter existing programs.

There are, then, three distinct aspects to the policy process: formulating the policy, establishing programs for policy implementation, and monitoring the effects of those programs. The monitoring process provides feedback to the leadership that helps to determine whether programs should continue, be changed, or be abandoned, as well as whether the policy needs to be altered. The foreign policy process takes place within a particular structure but has effects reaching throughout the world.

Rolling Thunder

Analysis from an organizational perspective offers certain advantages and, like any analytical approach, suffers from certain limitations. The limitations are derived primarily from the weaknesses of organization theory as a field of knowledge, which will be discussed in chapter five.

In the foreign policy arena a large number of organizations deal with a plethora of problems. When one approaches the concept of foreign policy from an organizational perspective, does one consider all of the organizations that are involved in the formulation, execution, and monitoring of foreign policy as one "mega-organization" or as a series of distinct organizations that are loosely related in the sense that they are all concerned with problems of national security?

Fortunately, the social science technique of model building allows some flexibility in dealing with this problem. A model cannot be used as an epistemological device, to define the basic, irreducible nature of the object; rather, it can be adapted to the operational situation confronting the analyst. In the science of physics, for example, electrons are treated as particles or as waves, depending on the theoretical situation. This variation is possible because there is no precise, universally accepted definition of electrons.[14]

And so must it be in this study. There is no universally accepted definition of an organization. At one level, we shall treat all of the individual departments, agencies, and bureaus of the United States government involved in the formulation, implementation, and monitoring of American programs toward Vietnam as if they were in fact one large organization composed of numerous sub-units. This organization will be referred to as either the national security bureaucracy or the command structure for Vietnam operations.[15] In other instances, we shall be concerned with the individual departments, agencies, or bureaus. And in still other situations, the focus of analysis will shift to sub-units of those individual organizations. The reasons for this change in emphasis from the mega-organization to the sub-unit of one of the individual agencies are dictated by the operational situation at hand. Some of the insights that can be provided as well as the kinds of issues that can be raised and examined from the organizational perspective emerge from the following description of part of the policy process with regard to Vietnam that occurred in 1963.

American policy toward Indochina was not formulated in an atmosphere of total agreement within the national security bureaucracy. Available evidence indicates that several groups within the bureaucracy held strong reservations about the idea that increased American forces would result in the eventual crushing of the insurgents.[16] The intelligence forecasts of the Bureau of Intelligence and Research (INR) of the Department of State, for example, repeatedly questioned the argument that continued expansion in aid and involvement would result in increased stability in South Vietnam. Yet the INR's forecasts that more involvement would not lead to a stabilized situation were largely ignored.

Why were these forecasts ignored? One hypothesis has already been suggested by the work of Janis: pressure of group norms among senior officials led to a discounting of the warnings.[17]

One example, however, demonstrates that other factors were at work. In the fall of 1963 analysts at INR produced a study that suggested that the war in South Vietnam was going badly for the Saigon government. Based entirely on classified statistical data issued by the Department of Defense, the INR memorandum also suggested that the statistics used to measure trends in the war were flawed by difficulties in obtaining accurate data. Using only the data from the Department of Defense, the analysts at INR came to conclusions about trends in the war that were vastly different from those of analysts at the Defense Department.

The pessimistic conclusions drawn by the INR analysts provoked acute protests from the Defense Department. Secretary of State Dean Rusk then apologized to the Joint Chiefs of Staff (JCS) for the State Department analysts' questioning of the analysis and data reliability of the Defense Department, and stated, "it is not the policy of the State Department to issue military appraisals without seeking the views of the Defense Department. I have requested that any memoranda given interdepartmental circulation which include military appraisals be coordinated with your department."[18]

Rolling Thunder

In practical terms, the Rusk directive meant that the secretary of state had directed analysts of the intelligence evaluation section of the Department of State—INR—not to question military appraisals in memoranda circulated to other branches of government without prior concurrence of the Defense Department. If INR analysts were unable to obtain concurrence, the circulated memoranda would reflect compromised views of State and Defense analysts. In short, sharp disagreements would therefore be muted instead of being allowed to surface and provoke debate.[19] The protest by the Defense Department did not center on which viewpoint was correct but rather on which agency or department had the right to analyze military data. Thus "substantive differences degenerated into a procedural issue."[20]

That the issue should turn into a question of organizational prerogatives rather than substance illustrates a disturbing point raised earlier. Ideally, disagreement between agencies should continue to surface at higher levels until resolution is achieved in terms of which agency viewpoint is more reliable. Instead, the issue was settled by requiring State Department analyses of military data to be coordinated with the military. In effect, official questioning of military reporting by the intelligence section of the State Department was ended about the same time that major escalation of American involvement was beginning.[21]

The response of the Defense Department also raises questions about how foreign policy organizations respond to challenges. When challenged, do organizations attempt to redefine the issue into a procedural question? What "causes" organizations to change existing programs if challenges from external groups are redefined into procedural issues?[22] How and when do organizations recognize that change is required because existing programs cannot achieve policy aims?

American policies failed in Vietnam because the most striking characteristic of these policies after the buildup of American forces was the imbalance between policy goals and the means available to reach those ends. American ends— preservation of the existing Saigon government and control of territory specified in the 1954 Geneva agreements in the face of a well-organized insurgency supported both externally and internally by a substantial portion of population within that territory—can be considered to be almost unlimited: That is, they required the restoration of the status quo, in which the Saigon government would suppress the insurgency and expel the North Vietnamese forces from territory claimed by the government of South Vietnam. The means available for pursuit of these ends were limited by two sets of constraints. First, domestic political opposition ruled out a general mobilization of the American population and economy. Second, fear of escalation into a vastly larger war with the People's Republic of China or a nuclear confrontation with the Soviet Union limited the kind of force that could be brought to bear in Indochina.[23] American policies failed, then, because of a basic contradiction between ends and means and an inability to abandon unattainable goals.[24]

It was the Tet offensive in January 1968 that laid bare this contradiction in an undeniable manner. After three years of battling the large American ground force and of receiving extensive punishment from air attacks, the insurgent forces launched an offensive that demonstrated they were not near military defeat. In fact, the offensive nearly broke the armed forces of the South Vietnamese, and it dramatically exposed the limited ability of the United States to control events. Following the offensive, there was a rapid growth of demands for change from within the United States.

Thus the phenomenon of organizational adaptation (or lack of it) to environmental realities is crucial to understanding why the United States continued combat activity well after a significant portion of the intelligence community was reporting that those programs would not succeed in achieving overall aims. The policy-relevant lessons will not be learned if the explanation is accepted that the Vietnam War would not have occurred had the United States been blessed with a different set of leaders. In a larger sense, an examination of the impact of organizational processes and politics upon policy formulation and execution in Vietnam is a step toward formulation of more general hypotheses about how public organizations function and why programs continue in the face of substantial information that they are not achieving their intended goals. But the organizational perspective that is taken in the next five chapters raises some questions of methodology and theory. In chapters two through four, the analysis will be primarily descriptive. There are two reasons for this approach. The first is to provide the reader with an account of what happened—how and why the United States began to bomb North Vietnam, how that program of bombing—code-named Rolling Thunder—was evaluated in terms of its goals, how evidence that the program was failing to achieve desired results was resisted by powerful groups within the United States government, how the failure finally became obvious to most (but not all) groups, and how the policy of strategic bombing was eventually abandoned by the Johnson administration. The second reason for the initial descriptive analysis is that a basis will thus be provided for the following examination of the theory of how organizations adapt or fail to adapt to external realities. In the epilogue, the short-term lessons about the effect of strategic bombing will be re-evaluated in light of the return to strategic bombing that took place during the Nixon administration as officials then in power searched vainly for a path that would permit "peace with honor." The concluding chapters strengthen the claim that organizational processes and politics are crucial, if not dominant, in the making, implementing, and measuring of the effects of foreign policy programs.

2. Rolling Thunder Begins

Foreign policy is formulated and carried out in an organizational setting. Issues, alternatives, and consequences are perceived, examined, and estimated according to the routines of the national security bureaucracy. The success or failure of a nation's foreign policy is therefore clearly influenced by the nature of the organizations that formulate and carry out that policy. In a like manner, military operations, as a component of foreign policy, are also influenced by the characteristics and routines of the organizations that implement them.

The next three chapters examine the formulation of the decision to initiate a sustained bombing program against North Vietnam; how the program, Rolling Thunder, was carried out between February 1965 and March 1968; and, finally, the nature of the feedback that permitted senior officials to monitor the program. Particular attention will be paid to the possible effects of organizational processes and politics upon policy.

The decision by President Lyndon Johnson in early 1965 to initiate a regular program of air attacks against North Vietnam was not actually a decision that represented a sharp break in or escalation of United States operations against North Vietnam. But to those unfamiliar with American actions in Indochina prior to the start of the regular bombing, the campaign appeared to be a significant escalation in American involvement. As we shall see, Rolling Thunder was the logical outgrowth of a series of efforts—some clandestine, others overt—that had been ongoing since at least 1961 and possibly earlier.

This chapter reviews how the operations conducted against North Vietnam led to a crisis in American foreign policy when North Vietnam PT boats attacked United States destroyers and how this crisis, in turn, closed off the options the president had been trying desperately to preserve. One of the major points here is that secret operations may initially appear to be highly attractive because they can be "denied" by officials in power. But such strategies can, and in this case did, backfire, and when they do, leaders are often forced into actions that they had been trying to avoid. Clandestine efforts may in fact cause more trouble than they are worth.

The Initiation and Consequences of Covert Operations against North Vietnam

On 29 April 1961, twelve days after the failure of the CIA-sponsored Bay of Pigs invasion of Cuba, President Kennedy approved an expanded program of covert operations against North Vietnam and an increase in American assistance for South Vietnam. The organizational resources available for clandestine operations in Southeast Asia, discussed by United States officials in detail, involved activities and personnel from the armed forces of South Vietnam, Thailand, Laos, Nationalist China, and the United States. Mercenaries from the Philippines were also part of the resource base.[1]

The organization charged with implementation of the program of unconventional activities against North Vietnam was created by detaching parts of the regular clandestine intelligence services of several national governments and charging each part with contributing to the overall operations. Private mercenaries from still another country were also involved. This ad hoc organization proved to be too unwieldy and was unable to mount a regular program of attacks. The structural characteristics of the ad hoc organization demanded that a large amount of organizational energy be devoted to coordination of the multiple units, which, even then, was poor. This example illustrates how the structure of an organization affects program implementation.[2] The operations against North Vietnam were unsystematic, scattered, and poorly coordinated.

A major question with long-range implications emerges at this point: what was the relationship between the covert actions undertaken against North Vietnam and the North Vietnamese infiltration of men and supplies into South Vietnam? Several facts are reasonably clear in retrospect.

First, the infiltration of men and supplies from North Vietnam into South Vietnam was highly publicized in the United States while the same sort of infiltration into North Vietnam was veiled in secrecy. Thus the American public (including most members of the legislative and executive branches) were not aware of American-sponsored activities against North Vietnam.

Second, the evidence is also reasonably clear that the insurgency in South Vietnam originated in 1957 and 1958 *without* significant support from North Vietnam. By 1959 and 1960, however, the growing North Vietnamese involvement became clear.[3] Thus by the time Kennedy approved the expanded program of covert activities in April 1961, North Vietnamese support for the insurgency was apparent. Fragmentary evidence, however, indicates that some covert activities against North Vietnam had occurred throughout the previous decade, thus predating the active involvement of North Vietnam in the insurgency.[4] A definitive answer to the complex question of infiltration on both sides and which series of actions triggered which set of responses will probably never be established.

At the same time, it is clear that senior decision makers were apparently unconcerned with this question. Covert operations were perceived as a means of signaling American intentions to the North Vietnamese without taking overt actions that would be subject to public scrutiny and debate. In short, covert operations offered the attractive opportunity of permitting one side to signal another without public involvement.[5] As will be shown, this attractive short-run tactic was purchased with hidden costs that became apparent only in the long run.

Rolling Thunder

In any event, the clandestine operations authorized in 1961 had no appreciable effect on the course of the war. The situation in South Vietnam continued to deteriorate despite the actions against North Vietnam and the expanded aid to South Vietnam. Thus, in 1963, "demands came—mostly from U.S. officials in Saigon and Washington and mostly because of the felt need to do something about a deteriorating situation—to increase the intensity of the covert operations and to change from covert to overt action."[6]

In May 1963, the Joint Chiefs of Staff directed the Commander in Chief, Pacific (CINCPAC) to prepare a plan for increased covert operations against North Vietnam. That the United States military instead of the Central Intelligence Agency was charged with planning the clandestine program was the outcome of the disastrous 1961 Bay of Pigs operation—an effort planned and directed by the CIA. Disgusted with the result of that operation, Kennedy had turned responsibility for such covert operations over to the military.[7] The result of the interagency struggle for control of clandestine operations following the Bay of Pigs was to have a major effect on the course of American involvement in Vietnam.

The plan that was to be drawn up by CINCPAC was set against the recognition that the situation in South Vietnam was growing worse and that the Saigon government might collapse.[8] The JCS rationale for increased covert operations was that they would raise the cost to the North Vietnamese of supporting the war in the south. North Vietnam, then, "faced with the credible prospect of losing its industrial and economic base through direct attack, would halt its support of the insurgencies in Laos and South Vietnam."[9]

The plan that CINCPAC prepared was approved in September 1963 by the JCS and designated Operations Plan 34-63 (OPLAN 34-63). After further discussion between CINCPAC and JCS, the plan was modified somewhat and redesignated OPLAN 34-A. Then, in December 1963 President Johnson directed an interdepartmental committee in Washington to review the proposal. After review, the president approved OPLAN 34-A on 2 January 1964. The process of drafting and approving the plan, in the face of the perceived worsening situation in South Vietnam, had taken eight months. Bureaucratic wheels ground slowly, even when the situation appeared to call for rapid action.

OPLAN 34-A called for a twelve-month program of covert actions against North Vietnam, including U-2 and electronic intelligence-collection flights, psychological operations such as leaflet drops and radio broadcasts, and twenty "destructive undertakings . . . designed to result in substantial destruction, economic loss and harassment."[10] Divided into three stages lasting approximately four months each, the levels of activity would be progressively increased.

There is no recorded evidence available that any organization or individual questioned just *how* a limited number of intelligence collections flights, a few psychological operations, or twenty "destructive undertakings" spread over twelve months would convince North Vietnam that its economic and industrial base would be destroyed. However, OPLAN 34-A did differ from earlier operations in two significant ways: the covert operations were formalized into a year-long program and operations were placed under the control of the United States Military Assistance Command, Vietnam (MACV). Clandestine operations against North Vietnam, previously organized in an ad hoc manner, were thus institutionalized. While the actual operations would be carried out by South Vietnamese or other non-American personnel, the "United States responsibility for the launching and conduct of these operations was unequivocal and carried with it an implicit symbolic and psychological intensification of the United States commitment. A firebreak had been crossed."[11]

A firebreak had indeed been crossed. OPLAN 34-A called for raids along the coast of North Vietnam by South Vietnamese gunboats. Coastal reconnaissance would also be conducted by American ships several miles offshore. On 2 August 1964, North Vietnamese PT boats attacked a United States destroyer engaged in one of these missions in the Gulf of Tonkin. The North Vietnamese may have mistaken the Americans for the South Vietnamese gunboats that were shelling North Vietnam a few miles away. Two nights later, a second attack was reported, and President Johnson ordered air attacks on North Vietnamese naval facilities in reprisal for the attacks on the

(above)
1. *On the night of 2 August 1964 North Vietnamese PT boats attack
the U.S.S.* Maddox *in the Gulf of Tonkin. This photograph was
taken during the attack from the* Maddox. *(Courtesy of the
Department of the Navy)*
(below)
2. *The U.S.S.* Maddox *at sea. (Courtesy of the Department of the
Navy)*

American ships. The action by the North Vietnamese and reprisal by the United States in August 1964, known as the Gulf of Tonkin crisis, set the stage for later American air attacks against North Vietnam.

To the public, most of the Congress, and most of the national security bureaucracy, the North Vietnamese actions were portrayed as unprovoked attacks on the high seas.[12] OPLAN 34-A covert operations led to the direct contact between the regular military forces of North Vietnam and the United States.[13]

In a second and more subtle way, another firebreak may have been crossed by OPLAN 34-A. The clandestine operations against North Vietnam included the use of so-called third-country personnel,[14] a term that refers to individuals from nations other than the nations primarily involved—in this case, the United States and South Vietnam. As has been noted, the clandestine program "resource base" included members of the armed forces and mercenaries from several other countries, as well as the United States and South Vietnam. In the summer of 1964, Chinese Nationalist guerrillas were reportedly trained by the United States in Taiwan and then dropped by air into North Vietnam.[15] At least some of the twenty destructive undertakings envisioned by the planners of OPLAN 34-A were carried out, then, by Chinese Nationalist forces.

The longer-range implications of the use of Chinese Nationalist guerrillas were apparently not of serious concern to those planners. Yet the use of these troops, part of the Nationalist Army engaged (albeit sporadically) with the Chinese Communist People's Liberation Army in the unresolved civil war for control of the Chinese government, could only have been considered provocative by the leadership of the People's Republic of China. The role of the use of these troops in the decision by the leadership of the People's Republic to provide extensive aid to North Vietnam can only be speculated. At that time, however, Secretary of State Dean Rusk was publicly suggesting that "Hanoi and Peiping have not yet learned that they must leave their neighbors alone. But this is a decision which they must reach."[16]

The record indicates that the use of Nationalist troops as guerrillas against North Vietnam was viewed as a routine part of the covert activities. Nationalist guerrillas were operating in Mainland China and in Laos and Burma, so why not in North Vietnam as well?[17] As in the case of the probable covert operations against North Vietnam in the 1950s, the exact relationship between these activities and the sequence of events that led to greater American and North Vietnamese involvement probably cannot be determined. Organizational activity, however, "does not constitute far-sighted, flexible adaptation to 'the issue' (as it is conceived by the analyst). Detail and nuance of actions by organizations are determined chiefly by organizational routines, not by government leaders' directions."[18] In short, the use of Nationalist guerrillas was probably consistent with the standard operating procedures of the unit charged with implementing OPLAN 34-A.

A variety of clandestine actions against North Vietnam such as those discussed above led to direct conflict between North Vietnam and the United States in the Gulf of Tonkin episode. Although OPLAN 34-A was initiated with the objective of applying pressure on North Vietnam in a discreet, yet undeniable manner, the options of escalation or disengagement were supposedly to be kept open for the future. The Tonkin Gulf reprisals, however, changed the nature of the available options. The American response, even though limited, reduced the number of options. Since the reprisal strikes were "accomplished with virtually no domestic criticism, indeed, with an evident increase in public support for the Administration,"[19] future attacks on American personnel and installations by opposing forces would have to be met with similar overt actions or the public posture of the United States would appear to be weakening.

Shortly after the air raids, United States ambassador to South Vietnam, General Maxwell Taylor, argued that the strikes were evidence of the American commitment and any compromise over possible negotiations would make the United States look like a "paper tiger." The Joint Chiefs urged additional actions to sustain the advantage gained. Assistant Secretary of State William Bundy felt that continuous military pressure coupled with some form of communication must continue. CINCPAC cabled that a relaxation of pressure would result in the loss of benefits gained from the reprisals. The arguments were summed up as "now that we have gone this far we cannot afford to stop and go no further; our original signal must continually be reinforced. What was not stated—at least in documentary form—were estimates of how long the process might have to continue or to what extent the actions might have to be carried."[20] In short, "the number of unused options short of direct military action against North Vietnam had been depleted. Greater visible commitment was purchased at the price of reduced flexibility. . . . The Tonkin reprisals were widely regarded within the Administration as an effective, although limited demonstration of the firmness of American resolve. However, they also served to stiffen that resolve and to deepen the commitment."[21]

The hidden costs of covert operations became clear. The unexpected had happened—North Vietnam had responded in an unanticipated manner. Instead of keeping options open, the covert operations had helped to close them off.

The Gap between Policy and Operations

In retrospect, one can see a wide discrepancy between what American leaders were talking about when they were concerned with the use of covert operations as a device to signal American determination and the actual conduct of the operations. Senior leaders were concerned with communicating intentions and saw the covert program as a means of that communication. The organization implementing the operations, however, could not translate this delicate nuance into action. Like all organizations, it functioned according to standard operating procedures (SOPs), which specify routines for accomplishing assigned tasks. A program—in this case OPLAN 34-A—is treated as a cluster of SOPs. Individual organizations, parochial in nature, develop programs for dealing with standard situations, and such programs may be ill-suited for handling situations that deviate from the "standard." Organizations are, after all, blunt instruments that tend to mash rather than slice.

Rolling Thunder

In the specific case of OPLAN 34-A, there were two aspects to the program: covert operations designed to inflict damage (and to threaten more damage yet) and intelligence collection (to assist in developing knowledge about weak spots in such areas as radar coverage). Thus the American destroyers were collecting intelligence. Since the most useful intelligence in this case could be obtained during actual combat situations, the standard scenario had intelligence being collected while the South Vietnamese (and Chinese Nationalists?) were inflicting damage (under the first goal of the program). The American destroyers were in the Gulf of Tonkin by virtue of the SOPs of OPLAN 34-A. The ships were located in international waters while the South Vietnamese gunboats were shelling North Vietnam. In the view of the planners in Washington and at CINCPAC, the United States ships were not violating any international law while collecting intelligence on North Vietnamese reactions to the actual attacks. Thus the American position, from the planning perspective, was legally sound and the reprisal strikes could be justified. As in so much of this sort of reasoning, however sound the case in the short term, the practical long-term implications tend to be discounted.

When the covert program was adopted by senior leaders, it ostensibly offered a chance to maximize gains—North Vietnam might be deterred, South Vietnamese morale might be raised, etc.—seemingly at a low cost. But while leaders were dealing with sensitive and complex problems of signals, the organizations were implementing a program based on standard operating procedures and pre-existing routines. The routines called for the use of "third-country personnel" and for American intelligence collection during actual combat situations. Then the unexpected happened and the hidden costs became more evident. When covert programs involve United States military personnel and equipment and those men and equipment are openly attacked, the ability of senior leaders to maneuver is dramatically reduced. It becomes important for leaders to understand that the routines by which organizations implement policy concepts play a critical role in influencing the future options of the leaders. Thus leaders must pay attention to the boring details of organizational routines. As Graham Allison has described in the case of the missile crisis in Cuba in 1962, this close attention will be resisted and resented by members of the organizations charged with implementation.[22] Such monitoring is a critical aspect of policy, however, and on it may hinge much of the program's success (or failure) in attaining the goals of senior policymakers.

Following the Tonkin reprisals, covert military actions against North Vietnam were resumed, the counterinsurgency effort in Laos was expanded by increasing support for the Royal Laotian Air Force, cross-border ground operations from South Vietnam into Laos were expanded without the knowledge of Laotian premier Souvanna Phouma, negotiations for the use of airfields in Thailand by the United States Air Force were recommended by American diplomats in Southeast Asia, and concern by senior United States policymakers was directed toward the expansion of United States facilities in South Vietnam for possible attacks on North Vietnam.[23] In addition, the JCS directed CINCPAC to prepare a set of reprisal targets in case future air strikes against North Vietnam were authorized.[24] And finally, in response to a series of questions from John T. McNaughton, an assistant secretary of defense, the JCS and the International Security Affairs Division of the Department of Defense replied that in the case of more aggressive North Vietnamese or Chinese Communist responses to the resumption of OPLAN 34-A operations, the United States should retaliate with reprisal air attacks including, if necessary, bombing Chinese Communist military bases if those bases were utilized for the aggressive responses.[25] The replies from JCS and the International Security Affairs Division did not suggest abandoning OPLAN 34-A operations in the face of increased reactions by the North Vietnamese.

When President Johnson decided to continue and in fact intensify the military pressures against North Vietnam after the Gulf of Tonkin incident, he acted on the consensus recommendation of his senior advisers. That consensus was, however, "achieved through a process of compromising alternatives into a lowest-common-denominator proposal at the sub-cabinet and cabinet level, thereby precluding any real Presidential choice among viable options. The choices he was given all included greater pressures against North Vietnam."[26]

At the same time, the consensus for increased military pressures, reached by compromise, did not reflect a common rationale among the president's principal advisers. A working group of the National Security Council was established to make recommendations concerning courses of action in Indochina. Chaired by Assistant Secretary of State William Bundy, the working group included Marshall Green and Michael Forrestal from the Bureau of Far Eastern Affairs of the State Department, Robert Johnson from the State Department's Policy Planning Council, Assistant Secretary of Defense John McNaughton, Vice Admiral Lloyd Mustin from the JCS, and Harold Ford from the CIA.[27] During the discussions, the representatives from CINCPAC, MACV, and the JCS favored heavy military action as a means of destroying the capacity of North Vietnam to continue the war. Maxwell Taylor, the United

3. *President Johnson and senior policymakers plan for the escalation of the war against North Vietnam at the LBJ Ranch in Texas, December 1964. (Photograph by Yochi Okamoto. Courtesy of the Lyndon Baines Johnson Library)*

States ambassador to South Vietnam, suggested continued air strikes as a means of improving South Vietnamese morale and of reducing infiltration. Walt Rostow, chief of the Policy Planning Council, emphasized continuing pressure on North Vietnam as a means of signaling American resolve. The civilian advisers to Secretary of Defense Robert McNamara and most of the other representatives from the State Department argued in favor of gradual increases in pressure (coupled with an offer to halt operations) as a means of compelling North Vietnam to give up its support of the insurgent forces. Only George Ball from the State Department dissented with the group recommendations of increased military pressures. The recommendations were offered in the form of options ranging from a slight increase in pressure to a massive aerial bombing program.

Consensus without Agreement: Policy and Program Implications

From the perspectives of the participants, the recommendations for increased pressure of varying degrees were seen as a means to differing ends. Although all members except George Ball were able to agree on a series of proposals, there was no agreement on the longer-range purposes of these recommendations. Thus, almost from the beginning, the program of increased military pressure was beset with disputes over exactly what it was to accomplish.

For the student of public policy, this is a relatively common phenomenon. In legislative politics, for example, a skillful party leader may be able to persuade members who have sharply different ideological perspectives to agree on a program. Each member is convinced by different sets of arguments and is left with somewhat different assumptions as to what the program will accomplish. The same strategy may be used in bureaucratic politics by advocates of a particular program to convince individual members of the organization of the potential benefits of the proposal. Daniel Moynihan, for example, reportedly used this strategy to convince a "conservative" President Richard Nixon to support the "liberal" Family Assistance Plan.[28]

Rolling Thunder

As the actual program begins to unfold, however, the original advocates of a program may find that it is not working as they expected. But by the time they begin to question the ongoing program, they find that the program has attracted other supporters and it becomes difficult to stop it. This is, in very general terms, what happened to the Rolling Thunder program.

In the short run, however, by concealing disagreements over ends behind a general consensus on means, the effective range of choice for President Johnson was limited. For the president to have chosen to reject all of the options proposed meant that he would have had to disagree with all of his senior advisers except George Ball.[29]

Through the duration of the actions against North Vietnam, this agreement on means and disagreement on ends by senior officials was to make it difficult for opponents of the action to criticize effectively the ongoing program. When the point was raised that a small program of clandestine actions would have little effect on North Vietnam's willingness to support the insurgents, proponents such as Ambassador Taylor could argue that it was necessary for South Vietnamese morale.[30] When critics suggested that covert actions would have only a marginal impact on infiltration, proponents such as Walt Rostow could justify the actions by saying that they were necessary to communicate the United States resolve to aid South Vietnam.[31]

Once the actions began, they were justified on multiple grounds that reflected the parochial priorities and perceptions of the participants and organizations involved. Ambassador Taylor, for example, was primarily concerned with relations between the Saigon regime and the United States government. For him, improving the morale of the regime to which he was representing the United States was of prime importance. To the Joint Chiefs, whose primary responsibility was the success of military operations against the insurgency, the program of action against North Vietnam could logically be seen as a means of reducing the military capabilities of the enemy. Because the program could be justified on differing grounds, some not conducive to validation through measurement, it was difficult to bring it to a stop.

After the decision to resume and intensify slightly the program of covert operations following the Gulf of Tonkin crisis, the JCS directed CINCPAC to prepare a list of targets in case reprisal strikes were ordered against North Vietnam. Various plans were drawn up, providing a range of choices from a few targets to be struck by a few planes to a large number of targets to be struck in hundreds of separate attacks.[32] This contingency planning is, of course, a normal part of the routine for any military organization. To have a set of plans "in the safe" does not mean that they will be used. However, it is likely that when governmental leaders decide to act, their choices will be constrained by the plans that *are* in the safe. Once contingency plans are established, military organizations will conduct training and familiarization operations, out of which organizational routines will be developed. These routines "for employing present physical capabilities constitute the range of effective choice open to governmental leaders confronted with any problem. The fact that fixed programs exhaust the range of buttons is not always perceived by these leaders. But in every case it is critical for an understanding of what is actually done."[33]

While the organizations within the United States were preparing for enlarged military operations, the political and military situation in South Vietnam continued to deteriorate (from the American point of view). In Saigon, a series of coup d'etats by military leaders had the effect of reducing the stability of the Saigon regime and, hence, its ability to prosecute the war against the insurgent forces. In the field, the strength of the insurgent forces continued to grow. At the end of 1964, "Hanoi held sway over more than half of South Vietnam and could see the Saigon Government crumbling before her very eyes."[34]

The Establishment of a Regular Bombing Program: Misperception, Misexpectation, and Momentum

As 1965 began, then, the covert programs had failed to deter North Vietnam but had reduced American options. As American perceptions of the situation in South Vietnam grew gloomier, a new rationale for air strikes emerged. The Gulf of Tonkin reprisals were intended as a one-time demonstration that American forces could not be attacked by North Vietnam. But by February 1965 retaliatory raids were to be made when United States forces were attacked by *either* North Vietnamese *or* insurgent military forces. An attack on Americans in South Vietnam was deemed sufficient reason for American attacks on North Vietnam.

In late January 1965 a patrol of navy destroyers similar to the patrols that were attacked in the Gulf of Tonkin in August 1964 was authorized. CINCPAC issued operations order Flaming Dart, which provided for air strike reprisal actions if the patrol was attacked. The first Flaming Dart mission was carried out on 7 February 1965, however, in response to an insurgent attack on American forces at Pleiku in South Vietnam. Thus, plans in the safe were used for contingencies different from those for which they were originally drawn.

An even more clear shift in rationale for attacks on North Vietnam became evident four days later, when the second Flaming Dart mission was launched. This air raid was not described as a reprisal for a particular incident, but rather as a response to a general pattern of aggression. The second Flaming Dart mission was an "air operation" rather than an attack. This new terminology reflected an expansion of the concept of reprisal in order to "accommodate a much wider policy of sustained, steadily intensifying air attacks—at a rate and on a scale to be determined by the U.S. Although discussed publicly in very muted terms, the second Flaming Dart operation constituted a sharp break with past U.S. policy and set the stage for the continuing bombing program that was now to be launched in earnest."[35] Thus air operations were conducted "against *North* Vietnam for offenses committed by the *Viet Cong* in *South* Vietnam."[36]

Against the background of the changed rationale and the worsening situation in South Vietnam, the decision to begin a sustained program of bombing against North Vietnam was made on 13 February 1965. The details of the program, code-named Rolling Thunder, were left vague because President Johnson wished to preserve maximum flexibility.

Yet his room for maneuvering was actually extremely limited. The United States was locked into an air war. Whereas covert operations had failed to strengthen the cohesion of the South Vietnamese government, the air campaign now beginning would serve that purpose—or so ran the argument from Presidential National Security Adviser McGeorge Bundy. Whereas covert operations had failed to deter or restrain North Vietnam from continuing its support for the insurgency, Rolling Thunder with its far higher risks of escalation into a war with the Chinese or the Soviets could accomplish that task—or so ran the argument from Ambassador Taylor. Whereas the covert actions had failed to present a believable threat against the small industrial sector of North Vietnam, a massive program of air attacks would perform that task—or so ran the argument from the Joint Chiefs of Staff, especially Air Force Chief of Staff General John McConnell.[37] In short, the same rationale was offered for the Rolling Thunder operations as for the covert program. Only the force levels and concomitant costs in terms of manpower and fiscal expenditures would be higher.

At the time of its initiation, advocates of the air operations program did not foresee that the program would last several years. Indeed, they expected quite the opposite, that Rolling Thunder would be needed for only a few weeks or, at the most, a few months. The Joint Chiefs of Staff, for example, proposed a program of strategic bombing that would last through the summer of 1965. A twelve-week program was thought to be sufficient.[38] This misperception among the agencies and individuals commenting on the advantages of the program probably contributed a great deal to its acceptability. As Allison has said, "Considerable misperception is a standard part of the functioning of each government. Any proposal that is widely accepted is perceived by different men to do quite different things and to meet quite different needs. *Misperception is in a sense the grease that allows cooperation among people whose differences otherwise would hardly allow them to coexist*" (emphasis added).[39]

In retrospect, the failure of senior American decision makers in the spring of 1965 to appreciate the weakness of strategic air power as a weapon must be judged as a colossal mistake in political-military judgment. How could these men so overestimate the effect of air power upon a determined enemy—an enemy that had fought and won a brutal war against the French? This question will be discussed in more detail in chapter three.

Because of continued political turbulence in Saigon (another coup d'etat was attempted, this time without success), the first Rolling Thunder mission was not carried out until 2 March 1965. The first six missions were operated on a one-at-a-time basis. After these missions, the strikes were scheduled on a weekly basis. Targets were listed that could be struck at any time during the week. Although the program was still limited by the number of sorties and the specific targets that could be struck, operational authority over when they could be struck had been delegated to the units carrying out the strikes. Rolling Thunder had become the regular program that its proponents had advocated.

When Secretary of State Henry Kissinger observed that "it is easier to get into a war than to get out of it,"[40] he was referring to the difficulty of stopping the momentum of national security bureaucracies and their ongoing programs short of clear-cut victory or defeat.[41] The gradual evolution of the clandestine activities from a series of scattered actions into a full-fledged program of covert operations and then the transformation of the larger covert program into a sustained bombing campaign illustrates one facet of the problem of momentum—the incremental growth of programs until they bear only general resemblance to the initial effort.

An examination of how the momentum for programs begins and then builds up will be helpful here. Rolling Thunder emerged after covert activities had failed to attain the various objectives for which they were designed. Yet how and why did the covert activities begin?

Widely attacked as immoral, illegal, and dangerous to democratic values, covert activities took on an increased importance in peacetime in early 1961 with the arrival of the Kennedy administration in Washington. Fear of escalation into nuclear war greatly restrained the behavior of the superpowers when in direct conflict with each other, especially after the nightmare of the Cuban missile crisis.[42] A widely shared view was that despite this nuclear stalemate, the Communist side, driven by messianic expansionism, had chosen to move from direct to continuing indirect challenge, through the device of guerrilla warfare.[43] Therefore the strategic doctrine of the United States had to change to place more emphasis on conventional and guerrilla warfare. American defense expenditures during the Kennedy administration reflected this emphasis, with spending for conventional and unconventional forces rising sharply.[44] The testing ground for Communist theories of expansion through guerrilla warfare was Southeast Asia.[45]

Within the region of Southeast Asia, the linchpin was South Vietnam. If South Vietnam fell to communism, the remaining countries of mainland Southeast Asia would soon follow. Extreme versions of this theory—labeled the domino theory after the analogy of dominoes toppling one after another after the first has fallen—posited the collapse of India to the west of Southeast Asia, Indonesia (and possibly Australia) to the south of that area, and the Philippines (and possibly Japan) to the north.[46]

In short, a series of interlocked and widely shared general beliefs were influencing policymakers at the time of the initiation of the covert activities program in 1961.[47] The point here is not to attack or defend these beliefs. Rather it is to note that when individuals deeply share a set of images, these images will heavily influence the decisions made. Those values act as a constraint on discussion and tend to push that discussion toward short-range questions about what options are available to deal with a problem rather than on fundamental assumptions. Thus many widely heralded "complete and thorough reviews" are really not that complete and are far from thorough. For example, in the decision to renew the covert activities after the Gulf of Tonkin incident, the fundamental assumption that the security of South Vietnam was vital to the security of the United States was apparently not examined. Since the participants held that general view, the discussions centered around *what* activities could be undertaken, not whether *any* activities at all were appropriate.

Rolling Thunder

Parochial priorities and perceptions, a key concept of the modern schools of organization theory, are less likely to be present when general values are threatened.[48] They emerge in debates over shorter-range options. Once programs are initiated, organizations charged with implementation tend to view those programs as useful and worthy of continuation or expansion.

When President Kennedy approved the expanded program of covert operations on 29 April 1961, he created an ad hoc interdepartmental task force to supervise and coordinate those activities.[49] Once the operations were underway, the regular departments and agencies involved followed the pattern of discovering (usually in the guise of program "evaluation") that those programs were promising.

The demands and pressures for expanded support that arose indicate how parochial priorities and perceptions of individuals and organizations lead to this imperialist tendency among those individuals and organizations. Organizations tend to define themselves in terms of budgets, manpower, and territory and attempt to maximize these characteristics. Individuals within organizations do likewise in a process known as "empire building." Individuals and organizations attempt to maximize their share of the action.

An additional source of pressure for expanded operations came from the interdepartmental task force set up to supervise and coordinate those activities. The ad hoc task force had been created to pay attention to the problem that senior leaders felt had been neglected, and it was seen as a way of providing information and alternatives that had previously been unavailable. The task force itself became an additional source of pressure, however, since "organizations created to provide an option also generate information and estimates that are tailored to make the exercise of that option more likely."[50]

The covert activities were authorized because of a general set of beliefs about the nature of the world. Organizational momentum began to build as the parochial priorities and perceptions and the inevitable tendencies toward imperialism combined. The interdepartmental task force emerged as a key source of pressure.[51] Once organizational momentum builds up, a program will not be halted at the point "where objective costs outweigh benefits. Organizational momentum carries it easily beyond the loss point."[52]

Because of the momentum that a program achieves, clear evidence that the program has gone beyond the loss point is required before that program will be terminated by the command structure. As we have seen, the covert program evolved gradually into the sustained program because it was not possible for opponents of the gradual expansion to demonstrate that the expanded program could not attain its objectives.

Summary

In this chapter, we noted that foreign policy is formulated in an organizational setting and that the characteristics and routines of the organizations influence the way issues are perceived, how policy is formulated, what programs are developed, how those programs are implemented, and how those programs are evaluated. In 1961, President Kennedy authorized a program of secret operations against North Vietnam. The program that was developed and implemented led directly to the Gulf of Tonkin crisis in 1964 and the beginning of Rolling Thunder. Instead of keeping options open for senior policymakers, covert operations closed them off.

In discussions by senior American policymakers, the general assumption was that it was important to deter North Vietnam from continuing its efforts to destroy the government in South Vietnam. Thus the questions facing decision makers concerned options (what to do) rather than assumptions (is it important that anything be done?). Once the covert operations began, pressures for expansion came from within the organizations charged with implementing them despite some evidence that suggested existing programs were having no effect. Apparently unless there is total and undeniable evidence that programs are not achieving objectives, momentum will probably result in increased levels of funding and activities. In the next chapter, we will observe these same phenomena at a far higher cost.

Before we leave our discussion of covert operations, one further point needs to be made. The American people were clearly deceived by their own governmental leaders, who made statements in the early 1960s picturing the North Vietnamese as the only side engaged in infiltration of men and supplies and other covert activities.

3. Rolling Thunder Fails

By 19 March 1965, Rolling Thunder had become a regular program of attacks upon North Vietnam, which continued until November 1968 when the peace conference opened in Paris. As a program of strategic air attack, Rolling Thunder was divided into phases. During each phase, a different emphasis was placed upon targets, and the scope and intensity of the attacks varied as well. And within the national security bureaucracy, extensive and intense infighting occurred over the program as intelligence information began to accumulate revealing that Rolling Thunder was not achieving its intended objectives. This chapter focuses on the program as it grew from a modest effort to an intensive air campaign designed to destroy North Vietnam's capacity to function as an economic unit and therefore support its forces in the south. It also details the internal strife that took place as a coalition opposed to the bombing formed within the bureaucracy. That coalition gathered strength as the intensity of the bombing increased until, in the summer of 1967, it appeared that Rolling Thunder might be drastically reduced or even ended. However, the coalition's efforts to scale down the bombing were blunted until the Tet offensive occurred in January 1968. President Johnson then joined the coalition and the bombing was first reduced and then ended. This chapter is not designed to chronicle what targets were struck at what time; that has been done in great detail elsewhere.[1] Nor will this chapter deal with tactical or battlefield aspects of the air war. However, the manner in which the organizational structure and routines constrained the strategic operations will be considered.

The Command Structure and the Beginning of Internal Debate

The gradual transformation of Rolling Thunder from a reprisal program to a sustained strategic air campaign is illustrated in table 1, which lists the Rolling Thunder mission numbers and describes authorized targets. Each mission had a number and assigned dates. Rolling Thunder 9, for example, was carried out between 2 and 9 April 1965. Within that period, a fixed number of air strikes was authorized for specific sets of targets within certain geographical limitations. In this manner, senior decision makers controlled the duration, intensity, and scope of the air campaign.

Air missions are classified broadly into strategic or tactical categories. Strategic air warfare is

> air combat and supporting operations designed to effect, through the systematic application of force to a selected series of vital targets, the progressive destruction of the enemy's war-making capacity to a point where he no longer retains the ability or will to wage war. Vital targets may include key manufacturing systems, sources of raw material, critical material, stockpiles, power systems, transportation, communication facilities, concentrations of uncommitted elements of enemy armed forces, key agricultural areas, and other such target systems.[2]

Strategic air warfare is therefore a long-term attack on the war-making capacities of the enemy. Tactical air warfare, on the other hand, consists of activities related to combat on the ground or at sea and is carried out "in coordination with ground or naval forces."[3] Within those broad categories are

Table 1
Evolution of the Rolling Thunder Program

Mission Number and Inclusive Dates	Targets	Type of Strike
Rolling Thunder 1[a] (20 February 1965)	A naval base and army barracks	Preplanned
Rolling Thunder 2–4[b] (February 1965)	Various targets in southern North Vietnam	Preplanned
Rolling Thunder 5 (2 March 1965)	Ammunition depot and a naval base	Preplanned
Rolling Thunder 6 (14–15 March 1965)	Various targets in southern North Vietnam	Preplanned
Rolling Thunder 7 (19–25 March 1965)	Radar sites, barracks, and ships along the coast as targets of opportunity	Preplanned, and armed reconnaissance
Rolling Thunder 8 (26 March–1 April 1965)	Radar sites, barracks, and targets of opportunity	Preplanned, and armed reconnaissance
Rolling Thunder 9 (2–8 April 1965)	Lines of communication in southern North Vietnam, including two bridges and vehicles using them (if military)	Preplanned, and armed reconnaissance

Source: Government Printing Office, "The Rolling Thunder Program Begins," IV.C.3, pp. xxiv–xxvi.
[a] Rolling Thunder 1 canceled because of political turbulence in South Vietnam.
[b] Rolling Thunder 2–4 canceled because of political turbulence in South Vietnam.

several types of air activities that may be used for either strategic or tactical purposes. (See table 2 for definitions.)

Aircraft involved in any one of these types of activities may operate alone or with other aircraft. A sortie is a single operation by a single aircraft. A mission is composed of several sorties. A flight of aircraft is normally composed of four aircraft operating together, and a standard mission involves four to five flights of four aircraft each for a total of sixteen to twenty aircraft. In a mission over the Hanoi area of North Vietnam, for example, twenty aircraft would operate together. Four of the sorties would be devoted to attacking and attempting to suppress anti-aircraft fire from the ground, four more would have the task of protecting the other aircraft from the enemy fighter aircraft (the "MIG CAP," or Combat Air Patrol), and the remaining twelve sorties would attempt to bomb the target.[4]

Rolling Thunder operations were composed of flights of aircraft engaged in strategic and deep interdiction missions. To conduct those missions, individual aircraft were also assigned to air superiority, aerial reconnaissance, psychological operations, defoliation, and reconnaissance by fire and were involved in both preplanned and armed reconnaissance strikes.

Authority to carry out the strikes was delegated from the White House and the Secretary of Defense to the Joint Chiefs of Staff on the basis of an approved preplanned target list that also specified the geographical area to be covered and the number and type of targets that could be struck in armed reconnaissance missions. The JCS then directed CINCPAC to execute the missions within the specified limits. CINCPAC, in turn, delegated the operational authority to units of the Pacific Air Forces (PACAF) and the Pacific Fleet (PACFLT). The PACAF units that participated in Rolling Thunder were part of the Seventh Air Force and were directed from Seventh Air Force Headquarters in Southeast Asia. Seventh Air Force aircraft operating within South Vietnam were assigned to the Military Assistance Command, Vietnam (MACV).

The same organizational structure was applied to the United States Navy forces operating in Indochina. Air units of PACFLT participating in Rolling Thunder were directed from the Seventh Fleet headquarters at sea (Yankee Station—about a hun-

Table 2

Types of Air Activities

Air superiority: The activity of first priority consisting of the destruction of enemy air capabilities including air and air defense forces and supporting facilities in order to gain control of the air for friendly forces.

Close air support: Air action against hostile targets which are in close proximity to friendly forces and which require detailed integration of each air mission with the fire and movement of those forces.

Interdiction, battlefield: To prevent or hinder, by any means, enemy use of an area or route; aimed at the logistic organization of the enemy already deployed in the battlefield area.

Interdiction, deep: To prevent or hinder, by any means, enemy use of an area or route; directed against lines of communication in the enemy's remoter base areas or against men and material en route to the area of operations.

Logistic air support: Facilitating the movement of men and materials into an area, often otherwise inaccessible.

Aerial reconnaissance: Tactical uses of air power to aid in location of enemy targets by visual, photographic, electronic or other means.

Psychological operations: Loudspeaker announcements, leaflet drops, and the like to communicate intended messages to enemy units of civilians for the purposes of affecting morale, etc.

Defoliation: Chemical attacks on the environment to deprive the enemy of the cover of vegetation, to deprive him of food resources, or to force the population of the area to move away.

Preplanned strikes: Air attacks, scheduled in advance, which aim at interdiction, strategic, or air superiority goals.

Armed reconnaissance: An air mission flown with the primary purpose of locating and attacking targets of opportunity, i.e., enemy material, personnel, and facilities in assigned general areas, and not for the purpose of attacking specific briefed targets.

Harassment and interdiction: An aspect of interdiction in which the effort is to disrupt enemy units.

Reconnaissance by fire: A probing attack on an area where enemy are suspected for the purpose of flushing out opposing forces.

Sources: All definitions are from Raphael Littauer and Norman Uphoff, eds., *The Air War in Vietnam,* pp. 17 and 19, except armed reconnaissance, from *Dictionary of U.S. Military Terms,* pp. 22–23.

dred miles offshore from Da Nang, South Vietnam) while those units providing support for activities in South Vietnam were assigned to MACV.

In addition to air force and navy units, United States Marines aircraft from the III Marine Amphibious Force occasionally became involved in Rolling Thunder as part of battlefield support activities when the marines were engaged in combat near the Demilitarized Zone (DMZ) separating North and South Vietnam.

Finally, when Strategic Air Command (SAC) B-52 or other aircraft bombed or engaged in reconnaissance in Indochina, they remained under the operational authority of SAC. These aircraft were controlled from SAC headquarters in Guam and, when B-52s were stationed in Thailand in 1967, from the SAC units at U Tapao Air Base in Thailand. Missions by B-52s were code-named Arc Light.[5] When MACV desired Arc Light support for operations in South Vietnam, it requested SAC to carry out the strike. Arc Light missions over North Vietnam were coordinated between CINCPAC and SAC. This seemingly confusing command structure is outlined in figure 1.

At this point it is important to note that all air activity within South Vietnam, with the exception of Arc Light, was controlled at a single point, MACV in Saigon. But air activity against North Vietnam was directed by military units physically removed from each other. Rolling Thunder operations were coordinated at CINCPAC in Hawaii. This organizational structure imposed limitations on both the conduct and the evaluation of the air war over North Vietnam, which will be explored in more detail at a later point.

The air war against North Vietnam can be divided into five phases. The first phase of Rolling Thunder began in the summer of 1965 with the objective of destroying the logistical system of North Vietnam and thus the capacity of the North Vietnamese to infiltrate men and supplies into South Vietnam. Attacks were concentrated on the infiltration routes in southern North Vietnam in mid-1965, but as the air war continued, the area authorized for operations was gradually expanded and targets were struck over most of North Vietnam. Prohibited from attack were most of the area of the cities of Hanoi and

Figure 1.

Command Structure for Vietnam Operations, 1965–1968

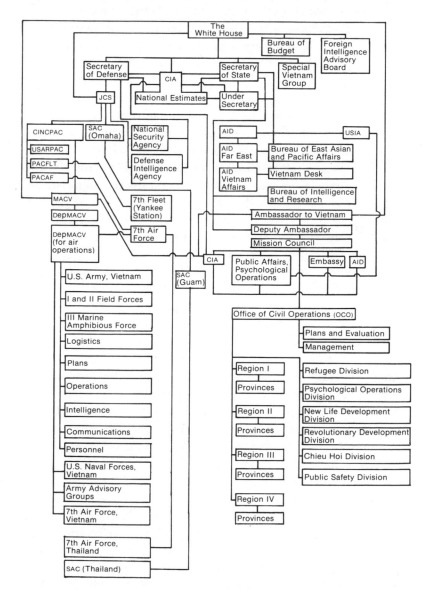

Source: Adapted from Walter Guzzardi, "Management of the War: A Tale of Two Capitals," *Fortune,* April, 1967, pp. 134–35.

Haiphong, as well as the area along the border between North Vietnam and the People's Republic of China.[6] Phase I of Rolling Thunder continued for the duration of the program.

The second phase of the air war involved an intense series of attacks on North Vietnam's petroleum storage facilities and lasted for about one month. Between 29 June 1966 and the end of July 1966, about 70 percent of those facilities were destroyed.[7]

The effects of these attacks were the subject of intense disagreements within the national security bureaucracy. Renewed pressure for escalation led to the third phase of Rolling Thunder. Phase III operations, begun in the spring of 1967 after the winter monsoon lifted, were directed against the industrial targets in North Vietnam including electric production facilities, the only steel mill in North Vietnam (located at Thai Nguyen), and a cement plant. Rivers and estuaries along the southern coast were mined. Targets along the Chinese border that had previously been off limits were also authorized for attack by President Johnson. By late fall, there were very few targets of any military or industrial value that had not been bombed and either destroyed or damaged.

Within the administration, debate about the value of Rolling Thunder became intense when the destruction produced by Phase III attacks failed to have a measurable effect on the war in South Vietnam. Thus when the insurgent forces struck throughout all of South Vietnam in the Tet offensive, a debate was raging within the national security apparatus over whether to escalate further (with options including destruction of the dikes and locks that prevented the Red River from flooding most of the heart of the North or a land invasion of North Vietnam) or to reduce the level of Rolling Thunder. The course chosen—to de-escalate—led to the fourth phase of Rolling Thunder. On 1 April 1968 the Rolling Thunder program was limited to an area south of the Twentieth Parallel; on 2 April 1968, a further reduction in the scope of the attacks to the area south of the Nineteenth Parallel was ordered by the president when CINCPAC ordered attacks just below the Twentieth Parallel a few hours after the de-escalation was announced. Phase

IV consisted of intense bombing aimed at interdiction in the area of North Vietnam closest to South Vietnam.

The fourth phase lasted until the beginning of the Paris Peace Conference in November 1968. After the conference began, air attacks on the north continued on a sporadic basis until 1972 during the fifth phase. Some of those attacks, called "protective reaction," reached levels of intensity comparable to the height of Rolling Thunder in Phase III.[8] Rolling Thunder operations are summarized in terms of sorties flown for Phases I–III in figure 2.

Before each of the phases was initiated, a debate took place in the national security bureaucracy. The outcome of that debate was reflected in the output of the national security apparatus—either an increase or a decrease in the scope and intensity of Rolling Thunder. The debate that led to Phase I was reviewed in the previous chapter. We shall now review the debates that preceded the initiation of Phases II, III, and IV.

Almost immediately after Rolling Thunder operations evolved into a sustained program aimed primarily at interdiction, pressures for escalation emerged. In April 1965, the chairman of the Joint Chiefs of Staff, General Earle Wheeler, suggested that the strikes had had virtually no effect upon the ability of the North Vietnamese to infiltrate forces in South Vietnam.[9] General John McConnell, air force chief of staff, argued in June 1965 that the only way to halt infiltration and thus reduce the ability of North Vietnam to support the war in the south was to conduct "an intensified application of air power against key industrial and military targets in North Vietnam essential to the results desired."[10] In July a study conducted jointly by the Defense Intelligence Agency (DIA) and the CIA indicated that the bombing had only marginal effect.[11] And in that same month, Secretary of Defense Robert McNamara concluded in a lengthy memorandum sent to the president that the effects of the bombing were not clear—with one striking exception:

> Morale in South Vietnam was raised by the initia-
> tion of the bombing program (as, later, by the deploy-

Figure 2.

Rolling Thunder Sorties: March 1965–April 1968

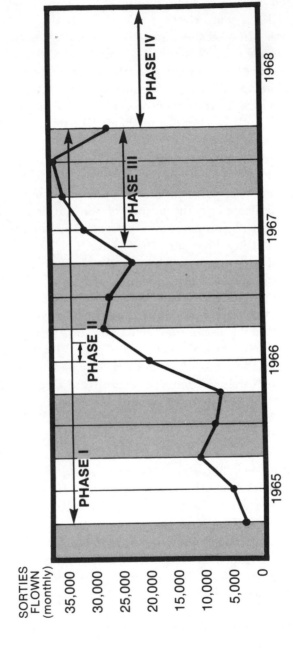

Source: Adapted from GPO, "Statistical Survey of the War, North and South: 1965–1967," p. 21; Littauer and Uphoff, eds., *The Air War in Indochina*, p. 44.

Note: Shaded areas indicate monsoon periods over North Vietnam.

ment of additional troops). Now—with the bombing programs having become commonplace and with the failure of the situation to improve—morale in South Vietnam is not discernibly better than it was before the program began. In a sense, South Vietnam is now "addicted" to the program; a permanent abandonment of the program would have a distinct depressing effect on the morale in South Vietnam.[12]

In three sentences, McNamara had stated a problem that was to be a major argument of those who opposed cessation of Rolling Thunder. The South Vietnamese tail had begun to wag the American dog. The threat to collapse was a powerful argument.[13]

Although the participants came to the same conclusion as to the value of the bombing effort, this did not mean that they would make the same prescription about how to improve the situation. To General McConnell, increased bombing would remedy the situation. But to others, here was a chance to cut losses before they became greater. At this point, participants could agree on the effects of the bombing but not on what to do about those effects or the lack of them. Later in the debate, the participants would not even be able to agree upon the effects of Rolling Thunder, a development that undoubtedly contributed to the acrimony of the later debate.

Some expected that merely beginning to bomb North Vietnam would turn the tide in favor of the United States. But those hopes were illusory and as spring turned into summer, American combat troops began flowing into South Vietnam to prevent the collapse of the army of South Vietnam. The debate about Rolling Thunder turned to strategies that would support those troops.[14] Within this context and given the administrative control mechanisms placed on the conduct of the operations by senior civilians in the command structure (limiting targets to weekly lists, fixing a ceiling on the number of sorties, etc.), the program grew in scope and intensity. The geographical area of authorized operations was expanded northward and the number of sorties authorized rose to more than five hundred per week, a 400–500 percent increase since the inception of Rolling Thunder.

In July, when air operations against North Vietnam were in their fifth month, the first major debate began. As the president was about to decide to triple the number of troops in South Vietnam, the under secretary of state, George Ball, sent a lengthy memorandum to the president and other National Security Council (NSC) principals. In that memorandum, "Cutting Our Losses in South Vietnam," Ball argued, "This is our last clear chance to make this decision [because] once we suffer large casualties we will have started a well-nigh irreversible process." [15]

But Ball was the only major NSC principal to take this stand. Secretary of State Dean Rusk's argument was almost the opposite. According to Rusk, it was crucial to prevent the collapse of South Vietnam because "the integrity of the U.S. commitment is the principal pillar of peace throughout the world. If that commitment becomes unreliable, the communists would draw conclusions that would lead to our ruin and almost certainly to catastrophic war." [16] To Rusk, saving South Vietnam had to be accomplished even at the risk of general war; general war had to be risked to prevent a higher future potentiality of one. [17]

Between the Rusk and Ball arguments, the remaining NSC principals supported a modest escalation. And the expansion of Rolling Thunder throughout the remainder of 1965 followed a step-by-step progression of geographical, target, and intensity increases. Between the "hawkish" views of the JCS and Rusk (and some congressional critics) and the "dovish" views of Ball, the president steered a middle course.

At the end of 1965 the Rolling Thunder program still had not produced the results intended. North Vietnam had not ceased its support of the insurgency nor did its will appear to be greatly affected.

In the North, the regime battened down and prepared to ride out the storm. With Soviet and Chinese help, it greatly strengthened its air defenses. . . . Economic development plans were laid aside. Imports were increased to offset production losses. Bombed facilities were in most cases simply abandoned. The large and vulnerable barracks and storage depots were replaced by dispersed and concealed ones. Several hundred thousand workers were mobilized to keep the transportation system operating. Miles of by-pass roads were built around choke-points to keep the system redundant. Knocked out bridges were replaced by fords, ferries, or alternate structures, and methods were adopted to protect them from attack. Traffic shifted to night time, poor weather, and camouflage. Shuttling and transhipment practices were instituted. Construction material, equipment, and workers were prepositioned along key routes in order to effect quick repairs. Imports of railroad cars and trucks were increased to offset losses.

In short, NVN [North Vietnamese] leaders mounted a major effort to withstand bombing pressure. They had to change their plans and go on a war footing. They had to take drastic measures to shelter the population and cope with the bomb damage. They had to force the people to work harder and find new ways to keep the economy functioning. They had to greatly increase imports and dependence on the U.S.S.R. and China. There were undoubtedly many difficulties and hardships involved. Yet, [North Vietnam] had survived. Its economy had continued to function. The regime had not collapsed, and it had not given in. And it still sent men and supplies into SVN [South Vietnam].[18]

The debate continued. An argument over a possible bombing pause produced two results. First, over the opposition of the Joint Chiefs, Rolling Thunder operations were indeed halted between 24 December 1965 and 31 January 1966. The second result, after the hoped-for negotiations failed to materialize, was the escalation of the air war into Phase II—the month-long campaign in the summer of 1966 to destroy the petroleum, oil, and lubricant (POL) production and distribution capacity of North Vietnam.

Where Phase I of Rolling Thunder had failed to halt infiltration or undermine the will of the North Vietnamese, the Joint

Chiefs of Staff pushed for expansion of the program by dropping the self-imposed restraints. Before the bombing halt, they had argued that Rolling Thunder was succeeding in making it somewhat more costly to support the insurgency, but

> we shall continue to achieve only limited success in air operations . . . if required to operate within the constraints presently imposed. The establishment and observance of de facto sanctuaries within the DRV [North Vietnam], coupled with a denial of operations against the most important military and war supporting targets, precludes attainment of the objectives of the air campaign. . . . Now required is an immediate and sharply accelerated program which will leave no doubt that the U.S. intends to win and achieve a level of destruction which they will not be able to overcome.[19]

What they could not overcome, according to the JCS, was a series of heavy attacks against the remaining military targets. If the whole package could not be struck, the POL targets were a minimum necessity since North Vietnam imported all of its oil and other petroleum products. Arriving by ship, these POL products were stored at thirteen locations. The North Vietnamese army used about 60 percent of those imports, and an attack would cripple the ability of that army by denying them the use of motor-driven vehicles and ships for the infiltration process. The North Vietnamese troops in the south, having increased to several regiments despite the bombing, required supplies that had to move by motor-driven vehicles. Furthermore, recovery would be difficult and prolonged. Since North Vietnam was already beginning to disperse its POL supplies by establishing alternate small distribution points, the POL targets must be hit immediately.[20]

Those views were not held by all members of the intelligence community. In the evaluation of Phase I of Rolling Thunder, there had been uniform agreement that the attacks had little effect on the course of the war. George Ball used that evaluation as part of his case for the cutting of losses. Ball based at least part of his arguments on work done by analysts within the State Department's Bureau of Intelligence and Research.[21]

But in the evaluations of the probable impact of the strikes on the POL targets reported in November and December 1965, there was disagreement among the various agencies. The Board of National Estimates of the CIA replied to an inquiry from Secretary McNamara, "We do not believe, however, that the attacks in themselves would lead to a major change of policy on the Communist side, either towards negotiations or toward enlarging the war."[22] A second study submitted to McNamara three weeks later by Richard Helms, acting director of the CIA, reinforced the earlier conclusion with the observation, "Although there presumably is a point at which one more turn of the screw would crack the enemy resistance to negotiations, past experience indicates that we are unlikely to have clear evidence when that point has been reached. . . . Though granting that each increase of pressure on the DRV [North Vietnam] bears with it the possibility that it may be decisive, we do not believe that the bombing . . . is likely to have such an effect."[23]

The Bureau of Intelligence and Research generally concurred with the CIA analyses. Thomas L. Hughes, the director of the bureau, noted, "As these attacks expanded, Hanoi would be less and less likely to soften its opposition and at some point would come to feel that it had little left to lose by continuing the fighting."[24] Hughes was arguing that the United States was holding the small industrial centers in North Vietnam as a hostage for the purpose of negotiations with the North Vietnamese. If, however, the hostage was destroyed, what would be left for the North Vietnamese to negotiate? For purposes of negotiations, the Hughes argument ran, the hostage must be kept alive because a dead hostage serves no purpose.

But the three service intelligence agencies, the DIA, and the National Security Agency (NSA) dissented from these views. They noted, in a footnote to the Special National Intelligence Estimate issued concerning the JCS proposal to escalate Rolling Thunder dramatically, that "as time goes on and as the impact of sustained bombing in NVN [North Vietnam] merges with the adverse effects of the other courses of action as they begin to unfold, the DRV [North Vietnam] would become clearly aware of the extent of U.S. determination and thus might reconsider its position and seek a means to achieve a cessation of the hostilities."[25] General Wheeler, chairman of the JCS, agreed with the dissenting opinion. A study by the JCS supported his view that bombing the POL system would be important in reducing the capacity of the North Vietnamese to support their forces in the South.[26]

The debate at the end of 1965 came to a temporary halt with the onset of the thirty-seven-day suspension of Rolling Thunder. The division in the intelligence community over this issue, however, must be noted. Those agencies closely connected with the military—DIA, NSA, and army, navy, and air force intelligence—agreed with the JCS estimates. The agencies identified more closely with civilian bureaucracies—the Bureau of Intelligence and Research and the CIA—raised important questions about the JCS arguments. Those questions went to the heart of the claims advanced for air power: even if the program were sharply increased, they implied, it would still have only marginal effects.

When the bombing resumed in February 1966, so did the debate. Another Special National Intelligence Estimate by the Board of National Estimates reached the same conclusion as that of the previous December. But at this point in the debate a puzzling second study by the CIA supported the JCS recommendations. This study, released in March, argued that Rolling Thunder had been ineffective because of "restrictive ground rules." North Vietnam was a "logistic funnel" through which supplies from China and the Soviet Union flowed. Interdiction as a goal was unlikely to succeed, and therefore Rolling Thunder should be directed at inflicting pain on North Vietnam. The targets that would cause the most pain were in the Hanoi-Haiphong area of northern North Vietnam.

Such contradictory evaluations emerging from the same agency within a one-month period point to only one conclusion. There was disagreement within the CIA over the bombing program and its effectiveness. Unfortunately, the exact dimensions of this split are not indicated in available documents. However, the more "hawkish" study was censored from the "official" version of the Pentagon Papers issued by the United

States government and can be found only in the "unofficial" version published by Beacon Press.[27]

The JCS and CINCPAC seized upon the new CIA study to press for further escalation. McNamara, who had rejected the JCS pressure, probably on the basis of the earlier CIA studies, now wavered and finally recommended escalation to the POL and other industrial targets.[28]

The president, however, did not immediately accept McNamara's new recommendation, probably partly because of the continuing hesitation of other civilian members of his inner circle. Those doubts centered on the possibility that those attacks might bring the Chinese into the war or push the North Vietnamese so far into a corner that they would fight as if they had nothing to lose.[29]

At the same time, an international peace effort was in progress, and it did not fail until June 1966. Other pressures were also upon the president. Within the United States, public opinion polls showed that support for the war had been declining steadily throughout 1966 and the Senate Foreign Relations Committee was holding lengthy, and sometimes embarrassing, hearings. Caught by cross-pressures, the president held off.[30]

The Escalation of Rolling Thunder amid Intensified Debate

By June, when the international effort to start negotiations ended in failure, the internal pressures for escalation apparently outweighed the external pressures against it and the president authorized the strikes for 24 June 1966; they were canceled after word leaked to the press. After instituting administrative procedures that kept the authorization messages out of the State Department, the attacks were again authorized as Rolling Thunder 50 and began on 29 June 1966. They apparently were successful; the storage facility near Hanoi was totally destroyed and the large facility near Haiphong was 80 percent destroyed.[31]

The debate over the escalation into Phase II revealed a

growing split within the command structure. Whereas the initiation of Phase I had had opposition only from the under secretary of state, George Ball, backed by the Bureau of Intelligence and Research, the debate over the initiation of Phase II indicated that the questioning of the program had expanded to at least part of the CIA—the Board of National Estimates—and at times included the secretary of defense, Robert McNamara.

Following the end of the POL attacks one month after their initiation, McNamara's earlier doubts over Rolling Thunder apparently became more insistent. The failure of Phase II to affect significantly the war in the south or to produce indications of North Vietnamese willingness to negotiate also played a role. From the initiation of covert operations against North Vietnam to the bombing of the POL facilities, proponents of escalation argued that the next step up the ladder would prove decisive. Each step, however, had failed to be decisive and the war was now extremely costly, with no prospect of ending. Although the POL strikes were a tactical success, they were a strategic failure according to CIA and DIA analyses.[32]

McNamara then requested a study of Rolling Thunder and the infiltration problem from a source outside the command structure—the Institute for Defense Analysis. The report submitted by some of the most distinguished American scientists hired for the study was bluntly critical of bombing as a means of reducing infiltration and inducing the North Vietnamese to halt their determination to see the war through.[33]

That study played a major role in McNamara's shift in views. Another probable factor in his disenchantment with Rolling Thunder was the increasing antagonism exhibited by domestic and international groups toward the national security apparatus.[34]

Using the findings of the scientists, McNamara repeatedly "pointed out to the Air Force and the Navy the glaring discrepancies between the optimistic estimates of results their prestrike POL studies had postulated and the actual failure of the raids to significantly decrease infiltration."[35] But the findings of the scientists did not merely criticize the existing program; an alternative was offered to the central problem of reducing the infiltration. The proposal was for the construction of an anti-infiltration barrier between North and South Vietnam and across the Ho Chi Minh trail in Laos as well. This alternative gave McNamara a crucial point of argument—that the main objective of the war was to prevent the collapse of the Saigon regime and that one of the means to that end needed to be changed.

With this alternative, McNamara joined the group within the national security structure who favored a halt in Rolling Thunder. In late summer 1966, after Phase II had failed, McNamara reversed his initial position and became an advocate of de-escalation of the air war.

McNamara's proposal for a barrier as a means of preventing infiltration as opposed to Rolling Thunder set off yet another round of debate within the United States government, which lasted from the fall of 1966 until the initiation of Phase III of the bombing in the spring of 1967 after the end of the monsoon. With the exception of McNamara, the protagonists were essentially the same. Favoring increased Rolling Thunder operations were the Joint Chiefs, Admiral U. S. Grant Sharp (CINC-PAC), and General William Westmoreland (MACV). This group was supported by George Carver of the CIA (who commented for Director Helms), the three service intelligence agencies and DIA and NSA. State Department reaction is not clear from available evidence, although Under Secretary of State Nicholas Katzenbach, who replaced George Ball after his resignation in the summer of 1966 (during Phase II operations), apparently supported proposals for intensified Rolling Thunder operations.[36]

Upon Ball's resignation, McNamara was the highest official supporting a reduction of Rolling Thunder. But he was a powerful advocate on the basis of his formal position in the hierarchy and also because of his personal characteristics.[37] McNamara was drawing upon the analyses of the Board of National Estimates of the CIA. The evidence that emerged indicating a split within the CIA over Rolling Thunder is strongly supported in the debate that followed the POL strikes.[38]

Thus the president was caught in the middle as the major

participants in the debate presented him with arguments for both escalation and de-escalation. As the debate continued until the end of 1966,

> the lines were drawn for a long fifteen month internal Administration struggle over whether to stop the bombing and start negotiations. McNamara and his civilian advisers had been disillusioned in 1966 with the results of the bombing and held no sanguine hopes for the ability of air power, massively applied, to produce anything but the same inconclusive results at far higher levels. . . . The military, particularly CINCPAC, were ever more adamant that only civilian imposed restrictions on targets had prevented the bombing from bringing the DRV [North Vietnam] to its knees. . . . The principle remained sound, they argued; a removal of limitations would produce dramatic results.[39]

As the new year began, a CIA analysis was somewhat supportive of escalation and a heavier bombing campaign that would include remaining modern industry and shipping, the Red River levee system, and other targets.[40] In early February 1967, the bombing was halted for the Tet holidays, over the protests of CINCPAC and MACV. During that respite Leonard Marks, director of the United States Information Agency (USIA), urged Secretary Rusk to extend the halt.[41] Externally, an international effort led by Prime Minister Harold Wilson of the United Kingdom encouraged the start of negotiations.[42]

That international effort failed. During the halt, the North Vietnamese made extensive efforts at infiltration of men and supplies and after the Tet holiday, Rolling Thunder operations were resumed. The target list for Rolling Thunder 54 included certain industrial targets, among which were the major steel mill and the cement plant. Airfields were added to the authorized lists for Rolling Thunder 55, and a thermal power plant was added for Rolling Thunder 56.

As the target list was expanded to include major industrial facilities, JCS forwarded a request from MACV for an additional hundred thousand troops for South Vietnam to be shipped immediately and for a hundred thousand more to be sent later.

This request confronted the president with another difficult decision—whether to escalate or to maintain the force levels in South Vietnam. To agree to the proposal would have meant mobilization of United States Army Reserves. The request set off another policy review.

Before he left for South Vietnam to direct civil operations, Robert Komer of the White House staff indicated he felt that more bombing of the north (including mining of harbors) would probably not be decisive. "This was the first time that Komer, whose preoccupation was pacification, had seriously questioned the utility of more bombing. Apparently the McNamara analysis was reaching even the more determined members of the White House." [43]

When most of the other senior White House aides made their views known, there were as many opinions as there were commentators. Another CIA evaluation of Rolling Thunder, in May 1967, this time was weighted in favor of the ineffectiveness of the bombing. [44] The JCS again advocated escalation. [45]

The debate continued into June as the courses of action narrowed to three alternatives. The first incorporated the essence of the JCS proposal for an intensive attack upon the Hanoi-Haiphong area, including the port facilities through which Soviet imports flowed. The second accepted the McNamara proposals for scaling down the air war and concentrating on the southern areas of North Vietnam, calling for a reemphasis on interdiction. This strategy was supported by the civilian secretary of the navy. The final alternative, supported by the civilian secretary of the air force, advocated a continuation of the present effort. The director of the CIA did not support any of the proposals because it was CIA judgment that "none of the alternatives is capable of decreasing Hanoi's determination to persist in the war or of reducing the flow of goods sufficiently to affect the war in the South." [46]

The apparent disagreement within the CIA was now resolved. The early view of the Board of National Estimates was shared by the director. The ambassador to South Vietnam, Ellsworth Bunker, added his doubts about Rolling Thunder: "Aerial bombardment, however, though extremely important, has neither interdicted infiltration nor broken the will of the [North

Vietnamese] and it is doubtful that it can accomplish either." [47] Bunker felt the barrier, proposed earlier by scientists from the Institute for Defense Analysis, was the best possible alternative. [48]

It thus appeared that the weight of the command structure was shifting away from escalation and toward some form of reduction. But the president made no decision, and Rolling Thunder 57 continued in the general pattern of the two previous segments of those operations.

At this point, Senator John Stennis of the Senate Preparedness Subcommittee announced that the subcommittee would hold hearings on the course of the air war. The list of witnesses scheduled to testify in August 1967 included all of the military officials involved in Rolling Thunder.

> The subcommittee had unquestionably set out to defeat Mr. McNamara. Its members were well known for their hard-line views and military sympathies. They were defenders of "air power" and often aligned themselves with the "professional military experts" against what they considered "unskilled civilian amateurs." They viewed restraints on bombing as irrational. . . . But more was involved than a disagreement over the conduct of the war. Some passionately held convictions had been belittled, and some members of the subcommittee were on the warpath. [49]

Thus, the JCS probably engaged in a tactic described by students of bureaucratic politics and foreign policy as "going to the Hill." Fearing that they were about to lose the internal debate on further escalation of Rolling Thunder, the JCS hoped to find support from the Congress and a means of creating pressure upon civilian decision makers, particularly the president. [50]

Pressure was indeed produced. Faced with the prospects of Congressional hearings in which military officials would appear one after another bemoaning the restrictions placed upon them, President Johnson expanded the list of authorized targets to include most of those for which the JCS had been press-

(above)

4. *President Johnson and senior policymakers meet to discuss the war, May 1967. These men met for lunch on Tuesdays and became known as the Tuesday Lunch Group. From President Johnson clockwise: Secretary of Defense Robert McNamara, Chairman of the Joint Chiefs of Staff Earle Wheeler, Press Secretary George Christian, National Security Adviser Walt Rostow, Vice-President Hubert Humphrey, CIA Director Richard Helms, Secretary of State Dean Rusk. (Photograph by Yochi Okamoto. Courtesy of the Lyndon Baines Johnson Library)*

(below)

5. *A North Vietnamese MiG is blown out of the sky, June 1967. (Courtesy of the Department of the Air Force)*

(above)
6. *U.S.S.* Constellation *aircraft attack an army barracks in North Vietnam, October 1967. (Courtesy of the Department of the Navy)*
(below)
7. *A-6A Intruder aircraft, heavily armed with bombs, in flight on a Rolling Thunder mission. The A-6A was one of the main aircraft used by the navy. (Courtesy of the Department of the Navy)*

8. *An F-4E fighter-bomber releases two two-thousand-pound
unguided bombs. The F-4 was one of the main aircraft used by the
navy and the air force for Rolling Thunder. (Courtesy of the
Department of the Air Force)*

Rolling Thunder

9. *A B-52 drops a string of bombs. When B-52s were used for Rolling Thunder missions, the operations were known as Arc Light. (Courtesy of the Department of the Air Force)*

10. *Admiral U. S. Grant Sharp, CINCPAC. Because of interservice rivalry, much of the coordination of Rolling Thunder took place at CINCPAC in Hawaii, 5,000 miles from the action. (Courtesy of the Department of the Navy)*

(above)
11. *As the bombing fails, President Johnson and the Tuesday
Lunch Group try to determine what to do. This photograph was
taken shortly before the Tet offensive in January 1968. (Photograph
by Yochi Okamoto. Courtesy of the Lyndon Baines Johnson Library)*
(below)
12. *President Johnson meets with Secretary of Defense Clark
Clifford and Secretary of State Dean Rusk. The president replaced
McNamara with Clifford when McNamara's doubts about the
bombing had become known to the public. At the time of this
photograph, however, Johnson had joined the coalition favoring a
halt on Rolling Thunder, March 1968. (Photograph by Yochi
Okamoto. Courtesy of the Lyndon Baines Johnson Library)*

(above)
13. *On 31 March 1968, President Johnson tells the nation that Rolling Thunder is being halted and that he will not run for reelection. The war had destroyed his political base at home. (Photograph by Yochi Okamoto. Courtesy of the Lyndon Baines Johnson Library)*
(below)
14. *President Johnson struggles with the burden of the war, July 1968. (Photograph by Kurt Kightlinger. Courtesy of the Lyndon Baines Johnson Library)*

ing. The tactic of "going to the Hill" succeeded and the president was outflanked.

Phase III of Rolling Thunder operations, like the other phases, had been preceded by an internal debate that eventually ended in escalation and subsequent evaluation that the escalation had not had much effect on the war in the south. During each debate, the coalition of participants expressing doubts had grown stronger. In the debate preceding the initiation of Phase III, the coalition had become so strong that it appeared that the bombing would be de-escalated.[51]

The coalition in favor of de-escalation did eventually emerge triumphant. Two key events turned the argument around—one outside the command structure and the other a change in the makeup of the internal coalition. The external event was the Tet offensive.

> The lesson of the Tet offensive concerning the bombing should have been unmistakably clear for its proponents and critics alike. Bombing to interdict the flow of men and supplies to the South had been a signal failure. The resources necessary to initiate an offensive of Tet proportions and sustain the casualties and munitions expenditures it entailed had all flowed in the south in spite of the heavy bombing in North Vietnam, Laos, and South Vietnam. It was now clear that bombing alone could not prevent the communists from amassing the material, and infiltrating the manpower necessary to conduct massive operations if they chose. Moreover, Tet demonstrated that the will to undergo the required sacrifices and hardships was more than ample.[52]

The internal event was that the president joined the coalition. The story of the president's change in position has been well documented elsewhere;[53] a few observations on the impact of the presidential reversal of view will be noted.

When the president joined the group favoring de-escalation, the weight of the coalition shifted dramatically. Policy changed, despite the efforts of the JCS to escalate the Rolling Thunder program even further.[54]

The policy change itself was not the result of a sudden shift within the national security bureaucracy. Rather, policy changed as a coalition formed, grew, and eventually became dominant. Thus Allison's finding that dramatic change occurs in response to major disasters does not adequately describe the "learning" process that occurred after the Tet offensive.[55] Although the change appeared to be sudden to the outside observer not acquainted with the internal struggles, it was in fact the result of the gradual emergence of a dominant coalition within the bureaucracy. As we have seen, the coalition had gained enough strength before the Tet offensive that pressure for de-escalation had almost triumphed. The effect of the Tet offensive was to accelerate the growth process of the coalition, not to trigger the sudden formation of a new coalition demanding a dramatic reversal of policy.

As each increasing level of force failed to produce desired results, the coalition favoring de-escalation grew. In short, the program failure triggered internal bargaining and pulling and hauling between individuals and groups within the national security apparatus. This activity, known as bureaucratic politics, was strongly influenced by the formal hierarchical structure of the national security bureaucracy. That hierarchy gave various players differential degrees of influence. Following the Tet offensive, only the JCS and most of the military remained dedicated to escalation. The development of the internal coalition is illustrated in table 3 and figures 3 through 6.

Two points are crucial here. The first is that those bureaucratic politics went on within an organizational setting. The second is that the coalition became stronger as the output of the organization failed to achieve intended results. That is, the participants in the command structure were reacting largely to events external to the organizational structure. Those external events took two forms: domestic political activity and the North Vietnamese resistance to manipulation.

Table 3

Principal Groups or Individuals Questioning Escalation of Rolling Thunder

Prior to Phase I	Prior to Phase II	Prior to Phase III	Prior to Phase IV
Bureau of Intelligence and Research	Bureau of Intelligence and Research	Bureau of Intelligence and Research	Bureau of Intelligence and Research
Under Secretary of State George Ball	Under Secretary of State George Ball	Secretary of Defense Robert McNamara	Secretary of Defense Clark Clifford
	Board of National Estimates (CIA)	Board of National Estimates (CIA)	Board of National Estimates (CIA) and CIA Director Richard Helms
		CIA Director Richard Helms	
		USIA Director Leonard Marks	Ambassador Ellsworth Bunker
		Ambassador to South Vietnam, Ellsworth Bunker	Robert Komer, Director of Civil Operations, U.S. Embassy, Vietnam
		Robert Komer, Special Vietnam Group	Senior Informal Advisory Group (many of whom were members of the President's Foreign Intelligence Advisory Board)
			Secretary of State Dean Rusk
			President Johnson

Figure 3.

Principal Groups or Individuals Questioning Escalation of Rolling Thunder Prior to Phase I

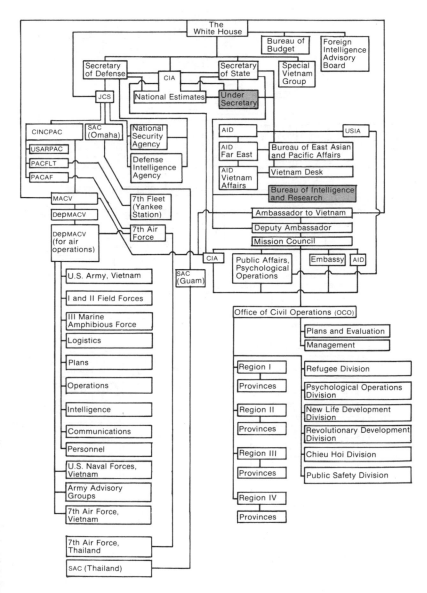

Figure 4.

Principal Groups or Individuals Questioning Escalation of Rolling Thunder Prior to Phase II

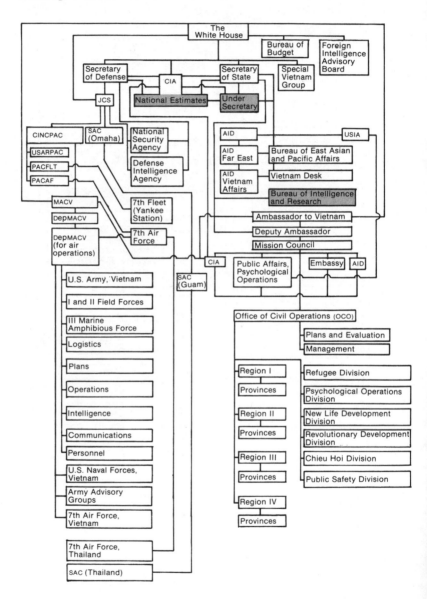

Figure 5.

Principal Groups or Individuals Questioning Escalation of Rolling Thunder Prior to Phase III

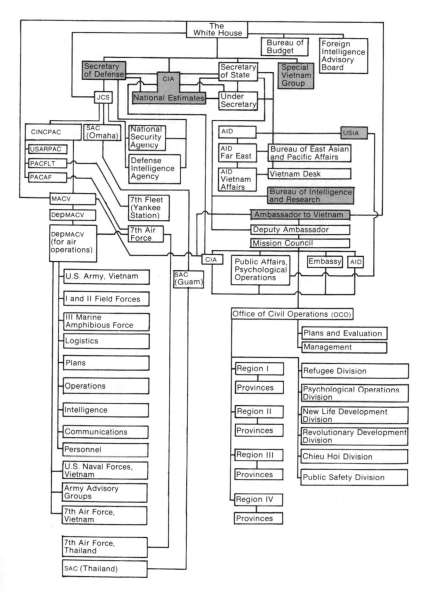

Figure 6.

Principal Groups or Individuals Questioning Escalation of Rolling Thunder Prior to Phase IV

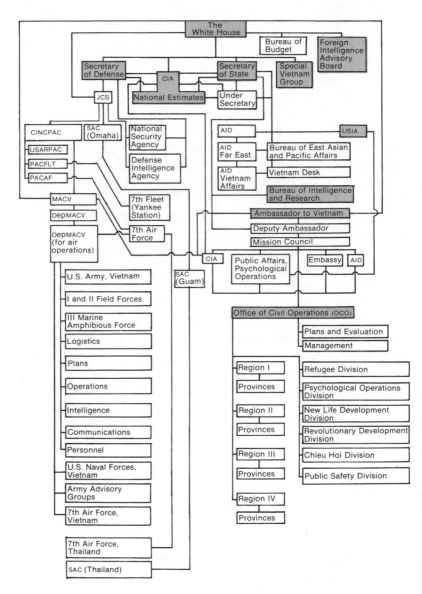

The Failure of Rolling Thunder

Students of bureaucracy have identified several models for understanding the behavior of large scale complex systems. Although these models will be discussed extensively in the last two chapters, a brief discussion of the bureaucratic politics model is necessary here to examine the question of why Rolling Thunder failed. In any bureaucracy, politics is an everyday occurrence. Those politics can occur over narrow internal considerations such as prestige, rewards, and status. Or, bureaucratic politics can be concerned with events external to the organization such as policy and program evaluations—that is, what effects are programs having on the target environment which is, by definition, outside of the bureaucracy. Each of these types of politics takes place, to be sure, but to what degree and under what conditions? As we examine the failure of Rolling Thunder, it will become apparent that it was difficult for some of the participants and groups to deal with the failure of the program in the external environment because the impact of failure would have internal bureaucratic consequences.

The initial reaction to the failure of Rolling Thunder (in Phase I) by the coalition dominant within the command structure was to increase the effort. As the costs of that effort rose, a second internal coalition unwilling to bear the burden, to pay the price emerged. That second coalition eventually emerged dominant and policy changed. But the central problem here still must be addressed: why did Rolling Thunder fail? The argument repeatedly offered by the JCS and CINCPAC was that "political restrictions" reduced Rolling Thunder effectiveness. This argument can be rejected immediately. Almost all of the restrictions were lifted during the end of Phase III of Rolling Thunder and almost every target of military value, as defined by the military, was attacked and either destroyed or damaged by December 1967. "Thus, except for the port of Haiphong and a few others, virtually all of the economic and military targets in NVN [North Vietnam] had been hit. Except for simply keeping it up, almost everything bombing could do to pressure NVN had been done."[56] One month later the Tet offensive was launched.

Rolling Thunder

The evidence against the JCS argument is so overwhelming that it bears no further discussion. But a second version of the argument, simply put, suggests that if the bombing campaign had been heavy in its early stages, North Vietnam would have collapsed. This argument is not based on evidence because there is none. It is speculation and must be treated as such. An equally speculative but equally forceful counterargument can also be offered: if the United States had launched a sudden and massive attack on North Vietnam in 1965, it might have been so shocking to North Vietnam's allies (i.e., the Soviet Union and China) that they might have become involved to save their ally. After all, the gradual escalation gave the Soviets and Chinese time to adjust to the fact of the program. Gradual escalation avoided a dramatic situation that they might feel compelled to resist. "There is no basis to saying with any certainty that air power unfettered by political considerations could have 'won' the war in Vietnam. Various outcomes of a more rapid escalation [were] possible, not all of them favorable to 'victory.' "[57]

What, then, contributed to the failure of Rolling Thunder? Part of the answer might be found by examining the kind of enemy that was being attacked and the theory of strategic bombing. Strategic bombing as a method of war emerged with the invention of the aircraft and was given its theoretical foundation with the work of Douhet.[58] A basic assumption of that theory is the existence of highly developed industrial bureaucracies that produce large quantities of weapons and supplies for utilization by armies in what Raphael Littauer and Norman Uphoff call "capital intensive warfare."[59] If those sources of supplies could be attacked and disrupted, the performance of the armies in the field would suffer.

But Vietnam could hardly be considered an industrial area. North Vietnam was an agricultural country with a primitive transportation system and almost no industry.[60] Furthermore, the North Vietnamese army did not follow conventional Western organizational forms, using large amounts of supplies. That army did not need to be supported with a huge logistics tail involving massive supply convoys and large supply bases. The supplies required for its operations were minimal and could be transported by a limited number of trucks, sampans, or coolies. Ironically, the primitive transportation system became an asset for resisting strategic and interdiction bombing. Paved roads for motor-driven vehicles were generally not required. Dirt roads used to support oxcarts could be repaired with a few shovelsful of dirt.

North Vietnam, in short, "did not seem to be a very rewarding target for air attack. Its industry was limited, meaningful targets were few, and they did not appear critical to either the viability of the economy, the defense of the nation, or the prosecution of the war in the South. The idea that destroying, or threatening to destroy [North Vietnam's] industry would pressure Hanoi into calling it quits seems, in retrospect, a colossal misjudgment."[61] Colossal misjudgments involve a misunderstanding of the theory that underlies the operation. Rolling Thunder was based on theories of warfare between industrial bureaucracies. Under conditions similar to those in Indochina, it is possible for a primitive nation to resist an industrial machine. Rolling Thunder failed, as did Operation Strangle in an attempt at interdiction during the Korean War, and these failures indicate that the theory is of only limited utility.[62]

But there was more to the failure of Rolling Thunder than a colossal misjudgment. Other factors were at work that made Rolling Thunder operations less effective than they might have been, even granting the absurdity of using expensive, technologically sophisticated aircraft to bomb a dirt road. The factors that may also have contributed to the failure have to do with the structure of the national security apparatus set up to deal with the problem of Indochina, which certainly influenced the conduct of Rolling Thunder and the effects of those operations.

The formal organizational structure of the apparatus, as shown in figure 1 (p. 41), reveals a major problem at first glance. Operations within South Vietnam, whether on the ground, in the air, or in the immediately surrounding waters, were supervised and coordinated, with the exception of Arc Light missions by SAC B-52s, by a single field commander on the scene, MACV (General Westmoreland). But there was no similar center of authority for Rolling Thunder, whose missions were carried out by two organizations operating semi-autonomously in the field. On the few occasions when Arc Light missions did strike targets in the north during Phases I–III, a third semi-autonomous organization became involved—SAC. The nearest point of coordination and supervision was CINCPAC, five thousand miles from the scene of operations. Sub-units of the command structure charged with carrying out Rolling Thunder operations are shown in figure 7.

Thus an admiring observer of the military command structure for Vietnam may have been a bit premature in his judgment that "from that apex at the White House run two long chains of command—one military, the other civilian. Appearances tend to deceive: the military chain is longer and looks more complicated, with its functional designations and its elaborate subordinations. But the military organization is very clear."[63] The second half of that assessment proved to be more prescient: "Everyone knows what his job is, and who his boss is, and everyone is trying to please his boss. On the civilian side, while the chain is shorter, entanglements begin almost immediately. Civilian jobs are harder to identify, and civilians have a propensity to talk back to their superiors."[64] We have already noted that the coalition to halt the escalation of Rolling Thunder began to take form in the civilian agencies. No major military representative or organization dealing with Vietnam supported that effort to de-escalate.

That there was no specific command for Rolling Thunder raises the obvious question: why? The most powerful explanation for this lack of a central command structure is built upon Morton Halperin's notion of organizational "essence." Halperin defines essence as "the view held by the dominant group in the organizational structure of what the missions and capabilities should be."[65] Operations in South Vietnam were oriented toward ground combat with enemy units, and air and naval units were subordinate to that purpose. Within the air force and the navy, the sub-units engaged in close air support, logistics, and transport were not part of the essence of those services. They thus could be subordinate to an operational commander from the service conducting most of the fighting—the army—without threatening the essence of the other services.

Figure 7.

Sub-units Charged with Rolling Thunder (indicated by shaded sub-units)

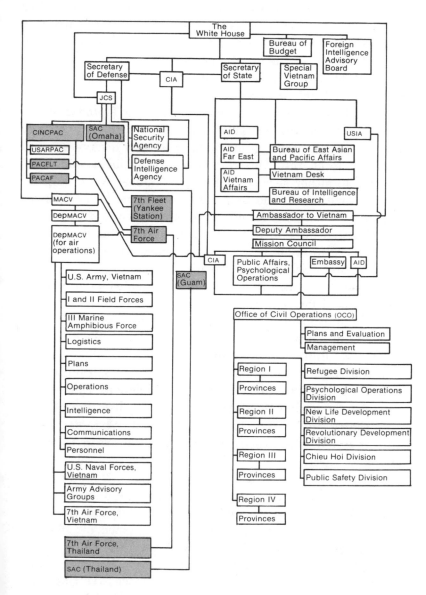

Rolling Thunder

But when air operations that involved strategic bombing were conducted, both the air force and the navy claimed them as one of their primary missions. Strategic air power is the essence of the air force and part of the essence of the navy. For forty years, the navy and the army air corps, then the army air force, and finally the air force have been engaged in an acrimonious dispute over the question of naval aviation for strategic purposes. Each has feared that the other was trying to capture its strategic bombing mission.

To establish a single command for Rolling Thunder operations meant that one service would have operational authority over the other: either an air force general or a navy admiral would be in charge. This command arrangement was unacceptable to either service. If Rolling Thunder went well, for example, with an air force general in command, the postwar dispute over aviation for strategic purposes would inevitably be influenced in favor of the air force. If the operations went poorly with an air force general in command, it would influence the postwar dispute in favor of the navy.

Interservice rivalry thus blocked the establishment of a single command for Rolling Thunder. Each service preferred to direct and control its own planes and personnel.[66] This exclusivism led to the organizational structure for command and control illustrated in figure 7.

As a practical matter, naval aircraft attacking from the sea were controlled and directed from the carriers at Yankee Station. Air force aircraft attacking from the direction of Laos were controlled from air bases in Thailand. When SAC B-52s were involved, they were controlled from bases in Guam or Thailand. Aircraft based in South Vietnam that were attacking North Vietnamese targets were controlled from a tactical aircraft control center at Da Nang, South Vietnam.

This elaborate arrangement meant that an enormous amount of organizational energy was consumed in efforts at coordination. Sections of North Vietnam, known as Route Packages, were authorized for naval aircraft bombing; other sections were designated for air force attacks. During each day's Rolling Thunder missions, aircraft attacked North Vietnam from different directions and were controlled at different

76

points. In order to prevent aircraft from one service from literally flying into aircraft from the other, each service would be restricted to attacking authorized targets in different Route Packages. To attack targets in one particular Route Package without flying into aircraft from the other service, fixed flight routines were established. The North Vietnamese air defense forces quickly learned where to concentrate their anti-aircraft forces by observing that aircraft entered and exited North Vietnam according to standardized procedures. Numerous additional examples might be given to illustrate how the interservice rivalry that prohibited the establishment of a single command influenced tactical considerations in the field.[67] Part of the reason that Rolling Thunder was less effective than it might have been is rooted in the problems at this administrative level. The inability of the Joint Chiefs to fashion a more effective command mechanism played a role in tactical considerations at which the military is supposed to excel but did not.

The argument that the administrative problems of organizing to conduct operations reduced the effectiveness of the Rolling Thunder program conflicts with earlier arguments that Rolling Thunder failed because a peasant-based agricultural system is, by its nature, resistant to aerial attack. Resolution of this apparent contradiction is important, because if one argues that a peasant economy is resistant to air attack, it makes little difference whether Rolling Thunder was carried out efficiently or inefficiently.

This latter conclusion cannot be supported, however. Because the operation of Rolling Thunder was conducted by a highly decentralized and only partially coordinated administrative apparatus designed by the services conducting those operations, the problem of effectiveness of air operations against a peasant-based economy is difficult to evaluate. Interdiction and strategic bombardment against such an economic system may indeed be a waste of time and money. One could also argue that a highly efficient and well-coordinated program might have produced more successful results. But because internal bureaucratic political activity prevented the creation of a centralized command structure, resulting in a poorly implemented program, one is left with the conclusion that peas-

Rolling Thunder

Map 1.

*Principal Air Force, Navy, and Marine Corps Air Bases
Utilized for Rolling Thunder Operations*

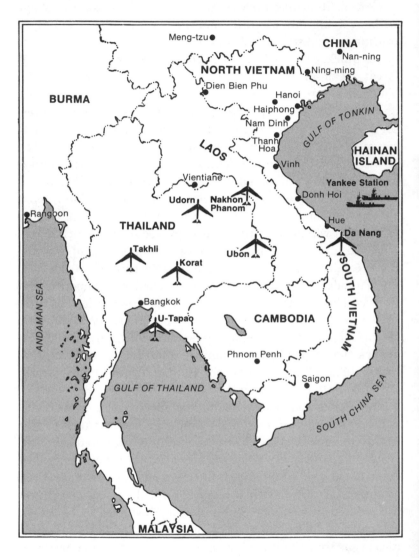

Map 2.

Route Package Areas and Operational Restrictions for Rolling Thunder

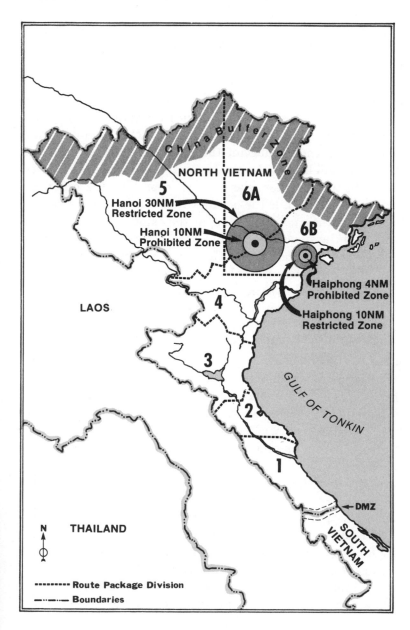

ant-based economies similar to that of North Vietnam (i.e., operating with a highly efficient authoritarian political structure and a strong nationalist fervor) are probably resistant to inefficiently conducted strategic bombing campaigns.

Furthermore, the interservice rivalry's influence on the organizational structure raises a problem for the student of organizational behavior and public policy. The bureaucratic politics described in this chapter influenced the nature of the policy decisions and the means by which programs are developed, implemented, and evaluated. Bureaucratic politics, in the form of interservice rivalry, also influenced the organizational structure for the conduct of the bombing. Furthermore, the internal struggle over the escalation of Rolling Thunder, noted earlier in this chapter, was shaped in part by the organizational structure. Thus the organizational structure influenced the bureaucratic politics while, at the same time, the politics influenced the structure. The question of why Rolling Thunder operations were conducted as they were cannot be answered by examining only the internal infighting (the bureaucratic politics approach) or only the organizational structure, rules and routines (the decision analysis approach discussed in more detail in chapter five). The two modes of analysis are not independent of each other.[68] Chapter six will provide a synthesis of the two approaches.

Furthermore, interservice rivalry also influenced the measurement of the effectiveness of the strategic air campaign. The measurement problem, which was the task of intelligence and other agencies, is discussed in detail in chapter four, but certain aspects of it should be mentioned here.

General David Shoup, a former commandant of the Marine Corps, recalled that "by early 1964 the Navy carrier people and the Air Force initiated a contest of comparative strikes, sorties, tonnage dropped, 'killed by air' claims, and target grabbing which continued up to the 1968 bombing pause."[69] A pilot who flew Rolling Thunder missions stated that "the result of all of this was that we were at one time sending kids out to attack a cement and steel bridge with nothing but 20-millimeter cannon, which is like trying to knock down the Golden Gate

Bridge with a slingshot. Stupid missions like that cost us aircraft and people."[70]

The above example illustrates "goal displacement," that is, the means to an end (goal) become the ends in themselves.[71] In the bombing, each service flew a number of sorties and dropped tons of explosives, with the goal of obliterating North Vietnam's capacity to support the insurgency in South Vietnam. However, the interservice rivalry created competition between the navy and the air force, each of which tried to fly more sorties or drop more bombs than the other and thus to dominate the strategic air mission. For example, aircraft were frequently flown with only a partial load of bombs or with *no* bombs at all in order to inflate the number of sorties. Thus, immediate military operations were in many ways subordinated to the long term struggle between the services for dominance of the strategic air mission.

Summary

The analysis of the strategic air campaign against North Vietnam has brought out several points with major implications for the study of organizations and foreign policy formulation and execution. The description of the internal debate within the national security apparatus indicates that the bureaucratic political activity surrounding the efforts to halt Rolling Thunder was triggered by the failure of the organization to attain organizational goals. The recognition of failure spread as the costs of failure mounted. But that recognition never occurred within the sub-units of the command structure charged with carrying out those operations. Failure was instead blamed on "political restrictions." Policy changed only when the groups opposed to the bombing within the national security apparatus could demonstrate that the program was failing to attain most of its objectives. When the disaster of the Tet offensive occurred, the president joined the coalition opposed to the bombing. With his critical support, the coalition became dominant and policy changed.

Rolling Thunder

That the navy and the air force were loathe to recognize the failure of Rolling Thunder should be no surprise. Recognition would imply that bombing had little military value and would have serious and pervasive implications for the organizations themselves and their tasks. Recognition of the need for change in the relationship between the organization and its environment and factors that prevented that recognition are the subjects of the next chapter.

4. Intelligence: Monitoring the Environment

It should be clear by now that widespread disagreement about Rolling Thunder plagued the agencies that formed the "intelligence community." This chapter will examine how such differing intelligence estimates could be produced. Two main points will help to clarify the discrepancy. In the first place, the indicators needed to measure adequately the effectiveness of Rolling Thunder were not available; without adequate indicators, the information that was produced was subject to widespread distortion, disagreement, and in some cases, deliberate falsification so that certain views and claims could be protected. Second, those agencies that did recognize that Rolling Thunder was not achieving intended objectives were organized differently from those agencies that did not recognize the program's failure.

The Problem of Constructing Adequate Indicators for Program Evaluation

All organizations, whether private or public, obtain resources such as people, materials, and money from the external environment.[1] The resources so obtained are then transformed into a product or service and exchanged with the external environment for new resources. To survive, an organization must have a favorable rate of exchange.[2]

In the conduct of public policy, the central problem is how to measure that exchange. A distinction between market (profit-oriented) organizations and nonmarket (governmental) agencies can help to illustrate the dilemma facing administrators of public agencies when they try to determine what they should be doing and to measure how well they are doing it. Market organizations, existing to maximize profits and minimize costs, are financed through the purchase of goods or services and by the sale of securities. The information flowing from the lower levels of the market organization to its higher levels is quantitative, concerning prices and costs and can be understood by nearly all members of the organization. Furthermore, the personnel of the market organization and the consumers agree on what is to be produced. The manufacturers of electronic equipment, for example, are not expected to produce lawn mowers. Thus, in one sense, it is relatively easy for senior managers of market-oriented organizations to determine what they should be doing and how well they are doing it. This is not meant to suggest that market-oriented organizations are exempt from disaster—indeed, a cursory review of corporate history reveals many examples to the contrary. But the point is that market organizations, in the main, do have a reasonably effective method of measuring performance. When a disaster, such as bankruptcy, does occur in a market organization, the student of organizational behavior generally accounts for that disaster with explanations that do not center on the ability of the organization to measure its performance.

Public organizations, on the other hand, such as the government, find it difficult to construct adequate indicators that will measure how well they are doing or even what they should be doing—because there is no agreement, except in the most general terms, between the customers (or clients or voters) and the government as to what the government should be doing. For example, while almost everyone in the United States would agree to the proposition that some effort should be made to provide an adequate national defense, there is widespread disagreement as to the implementation of that effort. Should we have a larger or smaller defense budget? Should we have more or fewer aircraft carriers? Should we have manned bombers or missiles or both? The general goal of the national security apparatus—to provide for the common defense—cannot be refined without inviting further dispute.[3]

The lack of agreement upon reasonably specific goals makes it difficult to agree upon specific programs. The descriptive analysis of the previous two chapters has provided extensive documentation of the disagreement over Vietnam operations. From the perspective of what should be done with Rolling Thunder, the command structure for Vietnam operations illustrated in figure 1 can be considered as a single organization composed of multiple sub-units. Those sub-units performed some common functions (e.g., the air force, the navy, and SAC engaged in Rolling Thunder) and some distinct functions (e.g., the air force engaged in close air support and defoliation, the navy performed maritime operations against infiltration of supplies and men into South Vietnam by sea, and SAC conducted heavy bombardment against large insurgent units or storage areas), but all interact with each other and with the external environment.

The output of the command structure as a whole may be considered to be American foreign policy toward Vietnam. But the output as a whole is not without some contradictions, because of the specialized functions of different sub-units. While the American embassy in Saigon, for example, was concerned with the pacification of villages, the Military Assistance Command was carrying out military operations that caused many of those villages to be destroyed or damaged.

Because of those contradictory aspects of program operations, measurement of how programs were functioning was a severe problem. Each sub-unit measured its performance according to sub-unit perceptions of what is important. No uniform system of measuring progress was devised for the whole operation, and that lack created a dearth of reliable data. Without those "sufficient statistics,"[4] only proximate criteria can be utilized—"that is, practicable tests which may not be necessarily or obviously consistent with ultimate goals. The fact that we use such criteria makes it easy to adopt erroneous ones."[5] If the criteria for measurement are erroneous, then the fact that the output of the organization is not achieving intended aims will be obscured until a very large gap has grown between what the participants think is happening and what is in fact happening. Some participants may never recognize that such a gap in performance exists.

When the program of action against North Vietnam was initiated in 1961, the participants in the command structure, as we have seen, shared little agreement on its goals. The same pattern characterized the decision to initiate Rolling Thunder after covert operations had failed to attain any of the intended objectives. Rolling Thunder was intended:

> a. *To promote a settlement.* The program was designed (1) to influence the DRV [North Vietnam] to negotiate (explicitly or otherwise), and (2) to provide us with a bargaining counter within negotiations.
>
> b. *To interdict infiltration.* The program was calculated to reduce the flow of men and supplies from the North to the South—at the least, to put a ceiling on the size of war that the enemy could wage in the South. . . . Supplemental purposes of the program were (c) to demonstrate to South Vietnam, North Vietnam, and the world the U.S. commitment to see this thing through, (d) to raise morale in South Vietnam by punishing North Vietnam, the source of suffering in the South, and (e) to reduce criticism of the Administration from advocates of a bombing program.[6]

Each of the phases of Rolling Thunder had different emphases, which suggests that the multiplicity of intended goals for the program left decision makers without a clear notion of what they were accomplishing. For example, Phase I operations were aimed at interdiction of infiltration, but Phase III operations were aimed at inducing the North Vietnamese to negotiate by destroying industrial and economic targets. Phase

III operations were also designed to reduce domestic criticism from advocates of air power.

Lack of knowledge about what was being accomplished was also aggravated by indicators that did not present an accurate picture of Rolling Thunder operations. In order to measure the effectiveness of the program, indicators were needed for each of the intended objectives. Program effectiveness can be measured, of course, only by comparison of intended objectives with actual results. When the indicators adopted tend to distort the actual results, then the feedback mechanism of the organization breaks down.

In the case of Rolling Thunder there was a discrepancy between indicators *required* to indicate effectiveness and the indicators *adopted* to indicate effectiveness. Within the command structure for Vietnam operations, certain sub-units recognized that the indicators adopted were distorting program results. Utilizing different indicators or analytical techniques, those sub-units challenged the validity of ongoing policy.

The indicators that were required to attain intended objectives are described in table 4. To achieve the six objectives, approximately fifteen indicators were needed, some of which were readily available and provided relatively accurate feedback. But some of them could not be developed and substitutes were adopted that introduced distortion into the feedback process.

To evaluate the success of the first objective in table 4, attempts to influence the North Vietnamese to negotiate, to break their will to resist negotiation, the existing diplomatic apparatus could be utilized and public statements of that regime could be monitored. Thus, throughout Rolling Thunder, the evidence that the North Vietnamese will to resist was never broken was easily obtained: they refused to negotiate.

The extent of the American commitment, the fourth objective in the table, was also easily measured in terms of manpower committed, dollars expended, and statements by American leaders stressing American will. In the end, of course, it was the fighting on the ground in South Vietnam that actually broke the will of one of the contestants.

Table 4

Indicators Required for Output Measurement

Intended Objective	Type of Required Indicator
1. Influence North Vietnam to negotiate by breaking the will to resist	a. Diplomatic communications indicating a willingness to negotiate b. Public statements indicating a willingness to negotiate c. Actions by North Vietnam such as halting infiltration
2. Reduce the flow of supplies and men being infiltrated	a. Measurement of the flow b. Measurement of men and supplies actually in South Vietnam c. Measurement of the North Vietnamese ability to produce or otherwise obtain those supplies
3. Place a ceiling on the ability of North Vietnam to infiltrate men and supplies thus limiting the combat capacity of the insurgents	a. Measurement of men and supplies actually in South Vietnam b. Measurement of the supplies required to conduct operations c. Measurement of the North Vietnamese ability to produce or otherwise obtain those supplies d. Measurement of the flow
4. Demonstrate U.S. commitment	a. Level of U.S. operations in terms of manpower committed and dollars expended b. Statements of U.S. leaders
5. Raise morale in South Vietnam	a. Measurement of morale over time among population and leadership
6. Reduce criticism of the administration	a. Measurement of criticism from other leadership groups b. Measurement of general public support

And measurement of criticism directed at the administration, the sixth objective, was also relatively simple. Public opinion polls and congressional demands served as satisfactory indicators.

The remaining three objectives—reduction in the flow of men and supplies, placement of an upper limit on the physical capacity to infiltrate, and an increase in the morale within South Vietnam—posed insurmountable problems of indicator construction partly because the data that could have measured these objectives simply could not be obtained.

Sources of Distortion in Intelligence Collection

Measurement of the South Vietnamese population's morale could not be accomplished over time in any systematic manner because of the combat operations throughout the country. Nevertheless, morale was "measured" on an unsystematic basis— through informal samples, discussions with leaders, interviews with local authorities—all techniques that were fraught with problems such as sampling error or purposeful distortion by respondents. These kinds of distortion are illustrated with the clear inference of goal displacement—means become ends—in the following observation by an official of the American embassy in Saigon: "And when you go to the smallest hamlet to see the Vietnamese hamlet chief, he'll have a chart. It's the new status symbol."[7] While the data on the chart may have been faulty, it would be presented on an official chart.

Accurate measurement of infiltration was also difficult because direct access to the infiltration routes was unavailable. Thus indirect measurement techniques had to be used, ranging from surveillance by aircraft and a limited number of ground patrols to electronic sensors and the monitoring of communications by units of the insurgent forces. The count of the men and supplies moving down the trail was at best only rudimentary. Was a truck convoy sighted in the afternoon the same one that had been sighted earlier in the morning further up the trail? Or were there two convoys? Did the sensing devices report the same convoy or convoys or was there still a third? Did the communications monitored indicate any units of the convoys involved or were the communications monitored part of different units? Did the information coming from the scouts along the trail duplicate information collected from other sources?

The technology of surveillance was based upon detection through sophisticated photography from aircraft (such as infrared photography), monitoring communications of insurgent units, visual surveillance by ground scouting teams, and electronic sensing devices placed along infiltration routes. From a technical viewpoint, the surveillance equipment was outstanding, including communications intercepts, sensitive photography, sensing devices, and scout reports. But the chief problem was assembling the reports from all of these sources into a coherent pattern that eliminated double counting and accounted for units missed by all sources. The task was made all the more difficult because the collection effort was fragmented among many American agencies and field units and reported along different channels of communication at different levels of security classification.[8] In addition to the problems confronting analysts attempting to sort out information from a bewildering variety of sources, evidence has emerged that intelligence was deliberately falsified by the military services in order to support military arguments that substantial progress was being made in the military effort to defeat the insurgent forces.[9]

Attempts to measure infiltration also took the form of collecting intelligence on the units operating in South Vietnam. What was their strength and where did they come from? A crude estimate could be made of infiltration by estimating the total strength of the insurgent forces at time t. The number of insurgents killed could then be subtracted and the number of local recruits added during time $t + 1$ should produce a new estimate of total strength if there had been no infiltration. If the number of insurgents was greater at time $t + 1$ than it should have been, the difference could be due to infiltration. But what if the number actually killed was lower than it was reported? Then the difference would be due not to infiltration but to inaccurate information on the number killed. Furthermore, what if there were great discrepancies between the total number of insurgents reported by one sub-unit of the command structure and the total number reported by another sub-unit? Then which was the actual count? This last question was not merely academic. Fragmentary evidence indicates that substantial disagreement existed within the command structure as to the number of troops in the insurgent units.[10]

Finally, the problem of estimating the amount of supplies required by the North Vietnamese to conduct operations was acute. As noted in chapter three, the North Vietnamese troops required far fewer supplies than did the American forces. Thinking in terms of their own supply needs, Americans therefore tended to overestimate the impact that destruction of North Vietnamese sources of supplies would have on the enemy's ability to continue operations. In a different situation, John Kenneth Galbraith noted the tendency to approach Asian problems from a Western frame of reference. The particular instance to which he was referring was a flood of the Mekong River and its supposed severe impact on the capability of the South Vietnamese: "I come now to a lesser miscalculation, the alleged weakening emphasis of the Mekong flood. Floods in this part of the world are an old trap for Western non-agriculturalists. They are judged by what the Ohio does to its towns."[11] In fact, the annual flooding of the Mekong had little effect.

The indicators that were adopted for the evaluation of Rolling Thunder and its ability to reduce infiltration or to place a ceiling on the amount that could be infiltrated reflected this problem. The theory of strategic bombing dictated that bombing could be effective if used in significant amounts. Therefore, two indices that would reflect the level of the effort would indicate damage and destruction and thus measure the effectiveness of the program. Those indicators were "sorties flown" and "tons of bombs dropped."

But those indicators have serious problems of accuracy. A sortie is a single operation by a single aircraft. Of a flight of twenty aircraft bombing in the Hanoi area, however, only twelve of them would be attempting to hit the target. The remaining eight were devoted to suppressing anti-aircraft fire and protecting the aircraft carrying bombs from North Vietnamese fighter aircraft.[12] In addition, other sorties had purposes of aerial reconnaissance, defoliation, and psychological operations. Thus, only about half of the sorties flown over North Vietnam actually involved attacking a target.

Of those, however, most were engaged in armed reconnaissance. In 1965 about 75 percent of the sorties were armed reconnaissance.[13] In 1966 less than 1 percent of the sorties flown were directed against targets on the Joint Chiefs of Staff target list.[14] Probably about 90 percent of the sorties were devoted to armed reconnaissance activities in 1967 during Phase III operations when the bombing was heaviest.[15]

Armed reconnaissance involves striking targets of opportunity as they become available. But when "significant" targets are not available, "insignificant" targets may be attacked. Admiral U. S. Grant Sharp of CINCPAC noted, "Sometimes people go out on an armed reconnaissance mission. They are not fortunate enough to find anything, and so then they let go on a less important target in order not to haul bombs back and drop them in the ocean."[16] Thus the total number of sorties flown does not indicate what targets were attacked nor does it discriminate between sorties for the purpose of attacking a target and sorties for other purposes. But the fact that most of the sorties flown over North Vietnam were of the armed reconnaissance variety does indicate that there were few fixed targets that were deemed important.

Using the number of tons of bombs dropped as an indicator also obscures effectiveness. When aircraft carrying bombs became engaged in a fight with a North Vietnamese aircraft, they had to jettison their bombs because the weight of the bombs slowed the aircraft and increased its vulnerability to the North Vietnamese fighter.[17] Bombs dropped at such times fell on targets not on authorized lists[18] and into swamps, rivers, and fields. The raw measurement "number of tons of bombs dropped" does not discriminate as to their targets.

Thus the two major quantitative indicators had serious reliability problems. The utilization of these indicators did have the effect, as we have seen, of orienting operational activity to the indicator that had been designed to measure attainment of objectives. Goal displacement influenced operations, as each service sought to fly more sorties and drop more tons of bombs than the other service.

Qualitative indicators were also subject to considerable distortion, partly because of the already noted tendency to approach the evaluation problem as if North Vietnam were an industrial nation dependent on the output of large bureaucracies. Another qualitative measurement was the observations of pilots engaged in Rolling Thunder operations. These reports, assembled during post-flight debriefings, were frequently submitted without the substantiation of aerial photographic reconnaissance. The summary reports were issued after the individual pilot reports were assembled but prior to confirmation through reconnaissance. Thus, one observer noted that targets reported as destroyed one day were frequently attacked the next.[19]

There was a little noticed, yet important, aspect to this type of reporting. If more than the actual damage was reported and those reports were accepted within the command structure, the only way to account for the continued flow of materials into South Vietnam was to assume that the North Vietnamese were importing large amounts of goods from external sources to compensate for the (supposedly) high attrition inflicted by Rolling Thunder. When Rolling Thunder pilots reported shooting down North Vietnamese fighters but large numbers of fighters were nevertheless continually observed on North Vietnamese airfields, the explanation produced was that Soviet or Chinese aid made up the difference.[20] Thus the indicators by which Rolling Thunder was measured were themselves subject to distortion problems. The indicators actually used are compared to those required in table 5.

The ability of the national security apparatus to monitor its environment was handicapped both by the lack of valid indicators for measuring performance, discussed above, and by the internal processes and politics operating within the command structure. For, once the information began to be transmitted throughout that structure, it was subject to influence by those processes.

Organization theory grew out of the early work of Marx and Weber. Weber described organizations in terms of their structure, and his approach continues to be central to the analysis of organizations. The fundamental concept of hierarchy as ap-

Table 5

Indicators Used for Output Measurement

Intended Objective	Indicators Used
1. Influence North Vietnam to negotiate by breaking the will to resist	a. Diplomatic communication b. Public statements c. Bomb damage estimates based upon sortie levels, pilot reports, and tons of bombs dropped d. North Vietnamese actions, such as increasing infiltration
2. Reduce the flow of supplies and men being infiltrated	a. Electronic, visual, and photographic surveillance, each subject to some distortion and reported by numerous agencies b. Electronic, visual, and photographic surveillance, espionage, and battlefield contacts, each subject to distortion, reported by numerous agencies and subjected to goal displacement c. Estimates of bomb damage based upon pilot reports
3. Place a ceiling on the ability of North Vietnam to infiltrate men and supplies, thus limiting the combat capacity of the insurgents	a,b,c. Same as for Objective 2 d. Estimates of required supplies obtained by determining how many men were in the south (this itself subject to distortion and disagreement) and then estimating need on the basis of what a Western army of equivalent size would need (with a "rule-of-thumb" subtraction such as: An American soldier weighs 160 pounds and requires so much food per day; an Asian soldier weighs 110 pounds and therefore requires 30 percent less)
4. Demonstrate U.S. commitment	a. Number of men in Southeast Asia (Vietnam and Thailand) and budget allocations b. Statements by executive and congressional leaders

Table 5–*Continued*

Intended Objective	Indicators Used
5. Raise morale in South Vietnam	a. Statements of Vietnamese leaders b. Subjective estimates of public support
6. Reduce criticism of the administration	a. Congressional and other elite opinion b. Public opinion polls

plied to organizations, describes the ranking among the participants within the organization in terms of rewards, status, and the right to make decisions. Decisions are made by senior participants and then passed down the organization through the process of delegation of authority as decisions move from the point of choice to the point of implementation. But modern organizations are characterized by a growing gap between the right to decide on the basis of hierarchical position and the ability to decide on the basis of technical competence.[21] Rapid technological changes have resulted in situations within organizations in which senior managers, having mastered specialties that are now obsolete, may indeed have the right to decide but not the competence.[22]

Growing tension within the organizational hierarchy as a result of conflict over the right to decide based on authority and the right to decide based on technical competence generates what Victor Thompson terms bureaupathic behavior. Bureaupathic behavior is characterized by greater attempts at control by superiors over subordinates, increasing dependence on formal regulations as a means of maintaining control, extreme aloofness in interpersonal relations, and resistance to change because of a fear that authority might be lost.[23] Presthus cites a form of bureaupathic behavior when he describes the ability of elites to control communication channels within an organization and thus make it difficult for an "unpopular" issue to move upward.[24] Wilensky comments on similar phenomena when he observes that in a hierarchy the rewards of power, status, and promotion—controlled by elites—are used to induce the accomplishment of work. Within a hierarchy, power is reflected partially by control over information. Thus the flow of information is subject to distortion through misrepresentation and concealment, as individuals attempt to maximize their power.[25] Crozier describes how groups in the French governmental bureaucracy use information and formal rules to preserve and, if possible, increase their power.[26] Such bureaupathic behavior is a prime contributor to the blockage of information flow within a hierarchy.

Why Did Recognition of Failure Occur in Some Sub-units and Not in Others?

Yet the description of the debate over covert operations and Rolling Thunder indicates that within the command structure for Vietnam operations, some sub-units recognized the need to change programs, but others did not. Therefore, if bureaupathic behavior is offered as an explanation, one must look for a distinction among the sub-units in the manifestation of hierarchy. That is, those sub-units that did recognize the need to change output must have had a less hierarchical form of organization.

Types of organizational structure have been outlined by Burns and Stalker.[27] Organizations that are mechanistically structured have an extensive hierarchy with communication flow primarily vertical. Loyalty and obedience to superiors and the organization are highly valued, and the formal leaders are assumed to be omniscient. A classic form of mechanistic organization is the military. If the armed forces were not organized along rigidly hierarchical lines with emphasis on loyalty, discipline, and obedience, they would be unable to function in a combat situation.

Survey research by Peter Karsten and his colleagues indicates that the attributes of loyalty, discipline, and obedience are present to a higher degree among members of military organizations than among the general population. In fact, the highest emphasis on these values was found among individuals who were graduates of the service academies.[28] Service academy graduates form the dominant coalition within each service and thus shape the essence of that organization.

A different type of organizational structure was recognized by Burns and Stalker for organizations operating under a different set of external conditions. In organically structured organizations, the interaction of organizational members resulted in continual readjustment and redefinition of tasks. Communication flow was more lateral than in mechanistically structured organizations because the communication content was directed more to consultation than to command and because the formal leader was not regarded as omniscient. There was a less rigid hierarchy and more direct information flow between members and leaders.[29] The attributes of mechanistic and organic structures are presented in table 6.

Any large-scale organization composed of many sub-units may demonstrate both mechanistic and organic structures in different sub-units.[30] The command structure for Vietnam operations certainly included both types of hierarchy. Let us return to the observation of that structure:

> From that apex at the White House run two long chains of command—one military, the other civilian. Appearances tend to deceive: the military chain is longer and looks more complicated, with its functional designations and its elaborate subordinations. But the military organization is very clear. Everyone knows what his job is, and who his boss is, and everyone is trying to please his boss. On the civilian side, while the chain is shorter, entanglements begin almost immediately. Civilian jobs are harder to identify, and civilians have a propensity to talk back to their superiors.[31]

Thus bureaupathic behavior tends to increase in organizations where an extensive hierarchy defines participants' actions and tends to decrease in organically structured organizations. Like most organizational attributes, its dimensions depend upon the degree to which other variables are present.

The shape of the hierarchy influences the information flow within it. The more levels through which information must

Table 6

Mechanistic and Organic Forms of Organization

Mechanistic	Organic
1. Tasks are broken down into very specialized abstract units.	1. Tasks are broken down into sub-units, but relation to total task of organization is much more clear.
2. Tasks remain rigidly defined.	2. There is adjustment and continued redefinition of tasks through interaction of organizational members.
3. Specific definition of responsibility is attached to individual's functional role only.	3. A broader acceptance of responsibility and commitment to organization goes beyond individual's functional role.
4. A strict hierarchy of control and authority operates.	4. There is less hierarchy of control, and authority sanctions derive more from presumed community of interest.
5. Formal leader is assumed to be omniscient	5. Formal leader is not assumed to be omniscient.
6. Communication is mainly vertical, between superiors and subordinates.	6. Communication is lateral between people of different ranks and resembles consultation rather than command.
7. Content of communication is instruction and decisions issued by superiors.	7. Content of communications is information and advice.
8. Loyalty and obedience to organization and superiors is highly valued.	8. Commitment to tasks and progress is highly valued.
9. Importance and prestige are attached to identification with organization itself.	9. Importance and prestige are attached to affiliations and expertise in larger environment.

Source: Condensed from Tom Burns and G. M. Stalker, *The Management of Innovation,* pp. 119–22 and Gerald Zaltman, Robert Duncan, and Jonny Holbek, *Innovations and Organizations,* p. 131.

pass, the more opportunities for distortion—intentional or accidental—of that information. In research on serial communication, W. V. Haney noted that, as the information flows through the hierarchy, details are often omitted, altered, or added because of the communicator's desire (1) to simplify the message, (2) to convey a sensible message (when the message is unclear, an individual changes it so that it "makes sense" to him), and (3) to make the message as pleasant or painless as possible.[32] When the information is communicated orally, these tendencies are aggravated by the increased possibility that the communicator will transmit what he views as the most important part of the message. In written communication, a communicator assumes that words are used only in the way he uses them, but to the individual receiving the information, the words may carry entirely different connotations that change the intent of the message. Haney cites the following written announcement as an illustration of the problem of unintended connotation: "Those department and section heads who do not have secretaries assigned to them may take advantage of the stenographers in the secretarial pool."[33]

Distortion of information, as described by Haney, is much greater when the information is non-quantitative, simply because its nonspecific character allows much wider interpretation and manipulation.[34] The information compiled in attempts to assess the damage caused by Rolling Thunder was non-quantitative (except for the estimated dollar value of the installations and supplies destroyed); thus the recipients of the information could read into the reports what they thought appropriate.

At this point doctrine (i.e., a set of principles) comes into play. As we have noted, air force and navy strategic doctrine posits the high value of strategic bombing. But when initial reports questioned the value of the Rolling Thunder program, doctrine was a block to that query. Herbert Simon noted, "For when a man is faced with ambiguity, with complex shadows he only partly understands, he rejects that ambiguity and reads meaning into the shadows. And when he lacks the knowledge and technical means to find the real meanings of the shadow, he reads into them the meanings in his own heart and mind, uses them to give external shape to his private hopes and fears. So the ambiguous stimulus, the ink blot, becomes a mirror. When man describes it, he depicts nót some external reality but himself."[35]

Recognition of the failure of Rolling Thunder was, then, blocked by doctrine, for the program failure confronted the Joint Chiefs with unpalatable alternatives. Rolling Thunder did not fail; it was simply not carried out properly. "The principle remained sound, they argued; a removal of limitations would produce dramatic results."[36] When the Tet offensive indicated that the intense bombing of Phase III had not had the intended effect, the JCS argued that Rolling Thunder must be continued at higher levels.

Finally, the internal rivalry between the air force and the navy that influenced the command structure for Vietnam operations also contributed to the distortion in the evaluation of those operations. In the long-run struggle over the question of which service would conduct strategic bombing operations, each service exaggerated the effects of its own operations.[37] An official of the American embassy in Saigon noted, "Management has become a great thing with the military. Westmoreland gives an order at 11:00 A.M. and in the afternoon there will be three colonels and two majors with the charts. They used to be only in black and white. Now they're in technicolor."[38] But it was the information on those charts that was crucial. That information, unfortunately, was distorted through accidental or deliberate efforts.

Summary

Intelligence, then, is not limited to the product from agencies formally charged with collecting information about foreign countries. Intelligence consists of knowledge about the organization and its environment, both its internal and its external attributes. In monitoring the environment, senior decision makers need to be aware of the effects of program output on the external environment. But they also need to be aware of the effects that internal characteristics may have upon the information as it flows through the national security apparatus. Inadequate indicators, distortion of information throughout the transmission process, and the structure of the organization itself all contributed to a delay in recognition that Rolling Thunder was not working.

The recognition of Rolling Thunder's failure by some sub-units triggered an internal debate that, as policy continued to fail at ever higher costs, led to the formation of an internal coalition that eventually became dominant within the command structure, and when it did become dominant, policy changed. The command structure for Vietnam then adapted to the external realities. It is to the process of adaptation and organization theory itself as a tool of analysis that we now turn.

5. Theory

This study focuses upon the impact of organizational politics and processes upon the making of United States policy with regard to the bombing of North Vietnam, the implementation of that policy, and the subsequent evaluation of whether or not Rolling Thunder was an effective program. The bombing program has been examined from its inception (as well as the covert operations that preceded it) to its maturity as a massive, deep interdiction, aerial assault designed to destroy the capacity of North Vietnam to function as a political, social, and industrial entity. At each stage of the escalation, individuals and groups within the national security bureaucracy opposed further increases. But recognition that the programs were not working was centered in sub-units of the mega-organization that were structured differently from the sub-units that never recognized the problem. The analysis up to this point has built up a body of information sufficient to allow us now to probe the central questions about the process of organizational adaptation or "learning."

Under what conditions do organizations adapt or fail to adapt to the environment?

If they are successful in maintaining themselves, is it because they learned from or manipulated the environment?

A review of work in the field of organization theory will help to answer these questions. Chapter six will provide a framework for understanding the behavior of complex, national security bureaucracies and a theory of adaptation (or "learning") for foreign and defense organizations.

The study of organizations and the impact of organizations on foreign policy can perhaps be best described as only partially developed. In the 1960s Karl Weick and James March noted the chaos in the field. Weick argued, "Any discipline will rise or fall depending on the reliability and validity of the observations on which its theories are based. Few fields have made so much of so little as has organization theory. The large number of theories, concepts and prescriptions far outdistances the empirical findings on which they are based."[1] March observed that "the literature leaves one with the impression that not a great deal has been said about organizations but it has been said over and over in a variety of languages. . . . There is a great disparity between hypotheses and evidence."[2] As late as the 1960s, then, organization theory seemed to be plagued by a plethora of unverified hunches, poorly tested hypotheses, partially examined problems, untestable propositions, and overgeneralizations.

Particularly important to note here is the fact that many studies of organizations done by social scientists used industrial organizations as their subjects. Nevertheless, those findings were often generalized to the case of governmental organizations. Within the recent past, however, some significant advances have been made in understanding how government organizations work and why they behave as they do. A basic point that has emerged is that, in many areas, government and industrial organizations are substantially different. Some of these differences will be explored in this chapter. Another fundamental problem of nearly all of the work until recently has been the inability of students of organizations to make the crucial distinction between analysis grounded in careful description and explanation, on the one hand, and analysis based on the normative views of the individual analyst, on the other.[3] Much of the analysis of American foreign policy by those who may be broadly categorized as "revisionists" is also damaged by this problem.[4]

Early Approaches to Organization Theory

The early literature on organizations was concerned with the impact of large-scale organizations on men and society. First Karl Marx and then Max Weber noted the development of industrial society and the accompanying disruption of men's lives and changes in their relationships to each other. As the size and complexity of industrial enterprises increased, Marx raised the question of whether bureaucracy was the master or the tool of policy. Marx's descriptive analysis was clearly influenced by his strong utopian view that early industrial society was intolerable in its dehumanization and exploitation of the workers in the industrial organizations. Marx's predictions about the collapse of capitalism and the rise of a utopian society in which large organizations would wither away sprang from this antibureaucratic viewpoint. His prescription to workers to overthrow the oppressive industrial state stemmed from a similar normative view.[5]

In contrast to Marx's normative, predictive, and prescriptive analysis, Max Weber attempted to describe bureaucracy without taking an antibureaucratic stand. Weber argued that one of the key characteristics (if not *the* key characteristic) of modern industrial society is the existence and operation of large, complex organizations. He then attempted to describe the characteristics of these organizations. Arguing that the industrial organization differed from earlier groups because it operated on the basis of regularized, impersonal, and legal procedures, Weber identified the crucial characteristics as hierarchy, specialization, advancement by merit, and differential power of the individual based upon his position in the hierarchy. These attributes, Weber suggested, were present in all modern organizations.[6] More recent research has suggested that all bureaucracies do not share equally all of the properties identified by Weber; rather the attributes are spread over a kind of continuum. Some organizations are less hierarchical than others, some have more detailed rules, some have more rigid requirements for promotion based upon merit, and so on.[7] Other research has challenged Weber's argument that bureaucracies are naturally effective and efficient by demonstrating that multiple-layered hierarchies may breed inefficiency.[8] Nevertheless, Weber's early attempts at descriptive analysis are fundamental to the study of organizations.

While Weber held that bureaucracies were effective and efficient in general, scientific management theorists argued that there was *one* best (i.e., most efficient and effective) way of organizing and accomplishing tasks. This idea marks scientific management as the predecessor to the more recent efforts of operations research and systems analysis. The theorists of scientific management, writing at the turn of the century and thereafter, saw their mission as finding that one best way, primarily through the method of time-and-motion studies in which an ideal time for task performance was calculated and the worker trained to do the job exactly as prescribed. Frederick Taylor and Frank Gilbreth are probably the best-known early proponents of the scientific management approach.[9]

Although scientific management theories were couched in the humanistic terms that increased efficiency in the factory would lead to more and lower-priced goods for all, the practical applications of scientific management were generally of a very different order. When discussing how the steel worker can be trained to load pig iron more efficiently, Taylor at one point describes the worker as "an intelligent gorilla" motivated only by a desire to make more money.[10] Workers were represented as automatons without personal needs, values, or concerns. Scientific management theories were mechanistic—men are machines that require proper maintenance—concerned not with describing organizations but with prescribing how to make them more efficient. Time-and-motion studies remain, of course, one of the major devices used along industrial production lines to achieve this goal.

Partially in reaction to the dehumanization of the workers as a result of the application of scientific management, another school of organization theory, human relations, arose after World War I. This approach also views the worker as a means of improving the efficiency of the organization. However, the needs, values, drives, and motives of the worker are of central concern; undergirding human relations theories are the assumptions that a happy worker is a good worker and a good worker will produce more. Borrowing heavily from psychological studies and methods, proponents of this school have prescribed methods to managers for handling their workers and thus increasing output.[11] Despite an inability to demonstrate a clear relationship between productivity and the high morale of the workers (some organizations do achieve higher productivity with more authoritarian types of management),[12] these theorists have continued to advocate management programs that have the underlying normative assumption that high morale will lead to high productivity. And despite the rejection of scientific management, the programs prescribed tend still to regard the worker as essentially a machine; only the type of oil to be applied to make the machine run smoother has changed.

Still another school of organization theory emerged following World War I. Growing out of Weber's early emphasis on organizational structure, the classical administrative theorists attempted to prescribe methods for improving production. Unlike Weber, they were not concerned with description and explanation. In contrast to the human relations and scientific management focus on the worker, classical administrative theorists centered their analysis on the structure of the organization. These prescriptions deal with how best to organize, coordinate, delegate authority, and specialize. Classical administrative theorists offered a set of principles that are supposed to increase efficiency and effectiveness. According to these guidelines, administrative efficiency is improved by: (1) specialization by group members; (2) limiting the number of individuals under the control of any one supervisor ("the span of control"); and (3) grouping workers according to purpose, process, clientele, or place.[13] While other theorists offered some additional principles, the core of the classical administrative approach is represented by these three major ideas. Even though advocates of the span of control may have disagreed about whether the proper number of employees per supervisor was five or seven, they agreed upon the concept of some ideal fixed number.

Despite Herbert Simon's devastating critique of classical administrative theory, now over thirty years old, classical administrative principles are still widely applied in both public and private organizations.[14] Management consultants earn lucrative fees for prescribing adjustments in the span of control or increased specializations. When the prescription results in further difficulties, additional fees are earned for discussing how the unity-of-command principle is now being violated. The United States Department of Defense, for example, is organized with the span-of-control principle as a key (if not *the* key) organizing device. This method has, naturally, resulted in a vast hierarchy. As some of the more recent findings have noted, many-layered hierarchies are prone to serious dysfunctions in processing information, coping with information overload, reacting to the environment, and resolving internal conflict. Part of the constant confusion and reorganization of both public and private organizations can be attributed to attempts to apply classical administrative principles. Despite wide recognition by more recent organization theorists that this theory does not adequately describe how organizations function and that the principles should be abandoned, senior personnel officers in many bureaucracies have been operating according to these rules for several years and are reluctant to discard them.

Classical theory also fails in the distinction between description and prescription. Nicos Mouzelis has noted that "very often, when one reads in textbooks on business or public administration about the functions of a department or of the executive, one is not sure if reference is made to what the executive does or what he should do."[15]

The vagueness of these early approaches to organizing accounts for much of the confusion in the field today. Analysts are still not really aware of the differences in types of analysis or of how normative assumptions and prescriptions may confuse description, explanation, and prediction. For example, consider the debate between proponents of these approaches over organizational goals. Classical administrative theorists must have a set of goals for the organization because without it, they cannot prescribe the appropriate organizing principles. Human relations and scientific management theorists must also have a set of goals for the same prescriptive purpose. In each of the early approaches, theorists assumed that organizations had a goal or set of goals that were widely shared and understood by the members of that organization—an assumption that leads one to describe large, complex organizations as if they were a cohesive unit. In fact, members of the same bureaucracy may have very different goals.

Modern Approaches

Current research has cast doubt on the idea that all organizations have a goal or a set of goals that are shared and widely understood by members,[16] although in some circumstances, it may be useful to view organizations in unitary terms.[17] More recent approaches that have attempted to describe and explain organizational behavior rather than to prescribe methods of organizing focus on either the processes within organizations, the structure of organizations, or the relationship of the organization to its environment. As Simon noted in his critique of classical administration theory, "The first task of administrative theory is to develop a set of concepts that will permit the description, in terms relevant to the theory, of administrative situations."[18] Organization theory has reached this point in its development only in the last fifteen years.

Decision Analysis

The first of the modern approaches—identified here as the decision analysis approach—attempts to describe the process of decision making in organizations. Investigators using the decision analysis approach begin with the empirical observation that wide discrepancies exist between an ideally rational decision[19] and the actual decisions that men and organizations make. Herbert Simon has been one of the major figures in attempting to develop models of organizational decision-making processes.[20]

Simon argues that a number of constraints on rationality exist and the decision-making process is influenced by these constraints. Of particular importance are the limitations on the abilities of individuals to process, store, and retrieve information. Citing extensive investigations undertaken by psychologists, Simon suggests that the distortions and errors that occur in the process of information storage, retrieval, and processing are major handicaps to ideal or rational decision making.

Similarly, Simon and his colleague James March note that pressures of having to make a decision within certain time limitations lead individuals to limit their search activities in problem solving. Rather than holding out for an optimal solution that may require extensive research, individuals will generally choose the first alternative that appears to satisfy the requirements of the moment. By this process of "satisficing" instead of optimizing, decisions are frequently made quickly, without realizing that some of the consequences will not be those intended by the decision maker.[21] Unintended consequences, of course, pose new problems requiring immediate attention (the proverbial "fire in the in-basket"), which are then also solved through satisficing decisions.

Richard Cyert and James March have added the notion that organizations are collections of subgroups, each of which has a different perception of what is important and what needs to be done. These divergent views, stemming from the parochial position of the individual participants in the organization, necessarily lead to conflicts; organizational decision making is thus frequently aimed at resolving conflicts between subgroups. Inconsistency in the behavior of the organization results in this process of satisfying the demands of first one group and then another because the demands are frequently contradictory or inconsistent.[22] From the perspective of understanding foreign policy decision making, it is critical to note that in this process of satisfying various groups, decisions that have consequences external to the organization are made on the basis of internal organizational needs and demands. What happens when decisions with external consequences made for internal reasons lead to disaster is not adequately understood. How does the organization respond?

Another source of constraints on rational decision making identified by analysts of the decision analysis school is the small group. Students of small-group behavior, beginning with Muzafer Sherif and Solomon Asch,[23] have suggested the "need" of individuals to see definite forms, patterns, or structure in events. "It was argued that for a certain class of situations, the small group serves to meet this need for a 'frame of reference' in a similar way by providing a major anchorage for the individual and his behavior."[24]

Small groups in and of themselves may or may not be harmful to the organization as a whole. In an article written over thirty years ago, Burleigh Gardner noted that small groups may exercise negative influence if the norms of the small group are in conflict with the larger purposes of the formal organization. And conversely, when the norms of the small groups are in accord with the larger organizational purposes, small groups may have a positive influence on organizational operations.[25] Janis, in his study of foreign policy and small groups, notes that in certain decisions (the Marshall Plan and the Cuban missile crisis, for example) the small group situation had a positive effect, while in others (which Janis labels "fiascoes"), the group decision-making process had negative effects on the overall outcome.[26]

The major characteristic of small groups that is pertinent to the study of foreign policy is the fact that groups place enormous pressure on individuals to conform to group norms; the individuals, finding the frame of reference provided by the group important, do conform under most circumstances or they are rejected by the group. Both the salience and strength of the pressures to conform and the individual's willingness and desire to conform have been extensively investigated and confirmed by social psychologists, as has the fact that groups tend to reject individuals who hold views that deviate from the norms of the group.[27]

Finally, other analysts have cataloged the dysfunctions of hierarchy, problems that result from the dilemma of centralization or decentralization as well as the rise of parochial views of the organization resulting from the extreme specialization required in large bureaucracies in order to solve complex problems. Their focus on the structure of the organization as a variable in decision making relates these analysts to the earlier classical administrative theorists. The critical point of divergence, however, is that classical administrative prescriptions were not based on any adequate description. It is the description of how the structure of the organization itself leads to differences between the ideal decision and the observed decision that sets more recent analysts apart from the earlier classical approach.

Harold Wilensky notes that, in a hierarchy, problems of coordination and the accomplishment of work are "solved" with rewards of power, status, and promotion—rewards that are controlled from the top of the organization. One key symbol of status and authority in bureaucracy is control over information. With this as a source of power, the hierarchical structure itself becomes a source of concealment and misrepresentation as individuals attempt to maximize their individual status and power. Subordinates tend to "play it safe" by not reporting problems, while superiors ignore subordinates in order to maintain authority. The growth of bureaucracy in the field of foreign affairs since the end of World War II has aggravated the problem, as large numbers of middle-level management positions have been created. These additional positions, necessary both to cope with the increased information flow and to provide specialists, have resulted in more filters through which information must flow and, therefore, in further isolation of senior decision makers.[28] In addition, the creation of a large number of middle-level positions has resulted in many-layered organizations with only a limited number of positions at the very top. The structure of the organization is extremely tall, with a pronounced narrowing at the top, a structure that provides a long promotion ladder for only a few individuals. Wilensky notes that "there are many time servers at the lower ranks who have neither information nor the motive for acquiring it. In the middle, among the non-mobile, there are many defensive cliques who restrict information to prevent change, many mutual aid and comfort groups who restrict information because of the resentment of more ambitious colleagues, and many coalitions of ambitious men who share information among themselves but pass on only that portion that furthers one or more of their careers."[29]

Much of the upward flow of information in large organizations (and especially in national security bureaucracies) is verbal because of the requirement that information arrive in time to be useful. As we have already recognized, details are often omitted, altered, or added because of the desire of the communicator to simplify the message, to convey a "sensible" message, or to make the message as pleasant as possible. Those who transmit the message may assign one meaning to a word or sentence while the recipient assigns another.[30] In a multi-layered hierarchy the problem is aggravated because of the numerous levels through which a verbal message must pass.

Hierarchy also permits the leadership to determine "what kind of issue will be raised for organizational consideration" because the elite controls the communication system whose "channels follow hierarchical lines."[31] This ability to control the content and style of issues raised increases the likelihood that issues not popular with the elite will not penetrate the hierarchy.

Another source of information distortion and blockage noted by Wilensky is specialization. Through specialization, a bureaucracy may draw upon a wide range of skills and expertise, thus overcoming the difficulty of limited human capacity for solving problems. Specialization, one of the primary characteristics identified by Weber, permits organizations to solve complex problems. At the same time, specialization inevitably leads to the development of parochial views about the organization and its problems by individuals and subgroups in the bureaucracy, causing them to focus only on the problem at hand and to feel that the specialized problem concerning them is the most crucial problem of the organization. In a larger sense, membership in any one organization for a long time leads to the view that the organization itself is crucial and that organizational programs must continue and expand.[32]

Finally, a third major structural problem is that of centralization. The dilemma of centralization/decentralization is simple: "plans are manageable only if we delegate; plans are coordinated in relation to organizational goals if we centralize."[33] The more organizations are centralized and controlled from a central location or management group, the easier it is to coordinate the operations of the sub-units of the organization but the harder it is to manage operations at the local level. Decentralization allows the "man on the spot" to deal with local problems but the disadvantage is that "the criteria adopted in lower-level problems will not be closely related to higher-level criteria."[34] As problems are broken down into manageable components and delegated, the criteria applied at the lower levels may not be compatible with the criteria desired by centralized management. In centralized operations, criteria may be standardized but may not fit every problem encountered at local levels.

The dilemma of to what extent to decentralize is not solvable in complex organizations that require central control and decentralized problem solving. Often a movement back and forth along the continuum between decentralization and centralization may be observed. In highly centralized organizations, management difficulties arise in dealing with specialized problems. In order not to disrupt the ongoing organizational operations more than necessary, centralized management may adjust slightly to solve the immediate problem by shifting toward decentralization. If the problem of management persists, further incremental movements toward decentralization may be made. Through a series of reorganizations, the organization moves toward the decentralized end of the spectrum. As the movement toward decentralization proceeds, problems of coordination begin to develop. To cope with these problems, incremental adjustments toward centralization are made. Thus large organizations engaged in solving complex problems typically undergo continuous marginal organizational changes. Within the organization, some sub-units may be moving toward decentralization while other sub-units are moving in the other direction. At any one point in time, then, organizational structure is changing and is in a state of tension between centralization and decentralization.[35]

Distinguishing between Market and
Nonmarket Organizations

Problems of centralization and decentralization are aggravated when a distinction is drawn between market (profit-oriented) organizations and nonmarket or governmental organizations. As we observed earlier, market organizations exist to maximize profits and minimize costs, and they are financed either through public purchases of goods produced or services provided or through the public sale of securities. The personnel of the organization and the consumers agree as to what is to be produced. The information flowing from the lower levels of the organization to its higher levels primarily concerns prices and costs and is therefore quantitative in form and understandable to nearly all members of the organization. These figures can be used as a means for senior-level managers to evaluate lower-level managers and to check lower-level organizational performance as a whole. Simon et al. notes that managers utilize accounting information to answer three kinds of questions: "Score-card questions—Am I doing well or badly? Attention-directing questions—What problems should I look into? Problem-solving questions—Of the several ways of doing the job, which is best?"[36]

Because managers in market organizations have a standard (profits and costs) for evaluating their decisions, it becomes possible for them to structure the situation so that lower-level managers will operate within the general instructions set by higher management. Thus headquarters delegates "authority over a wide range of decisions. This delegation drastically reduces the information which must flow"[37] from the lower units to headquarters. Headquarters, in turn, can check on the performance of the lower units and thus mitigate some of the biases in the performance reports of lower levels. When Cyert and March argue that "despite bias in communication introduced . . . the system does not become hopelessly confused," they are speaking of market organizations.[38]

Reliable performance checks cannot be accomplished in governmental organizations to the same extent. While market organizations have an agreed-upon set of goals (maximization of profits and minimization of costs), there is substantial disagreement over the goals of governmental organizations. In market organizations, prices and costs serve as a set of "sufficient statistics" that measure performance. No such set of sufficient statistics can be developed in organizations where there is a lack of agreement about what the organization should be doing. As McKean has noted,

> In comparing alternate government operations or courses of action, we cannot apply what might be called ultimate criteria. Thus we cannot apply such tests as "maximum well-being from available resources." Without more precise definitions, this is merely saying that we want the best. And when we spell out tests of preferredness more precisely, we find that we are using proximate criteria—that is, practicable tests which are not necessarily or obviously consistent with ultimate goals. The fact that we use such criteria makes it easy to adopt erroneous ones.[39]

As a result of the use of proximate criteria, output measurement is a major problem for nonmarket organizations. Senior nonmarket decision makers do not usually have effective means of verifying the quality of performance from reports flowing up the organization from lower levels. Since there is no agreed-upon method of measuring performance, it is difficult for leadership to structure the situation so that lower levels will perform in the desired manner. Thus, public organizations are differentiated from private market organizations in two extremely important ways: the lack of agreement about what the organization should be doing and difficulties in constructing adequate indicators to measure output. These, of course, are the same problems faced by decision makers when they were attempting to formulate, implement, and evaluate policies directed against North Vietnam. It should be reasonably clear by now that the absence of adequate indicators and disputes over what should be done meant that *there was no one best way to organize.* Regardless of how the organization was structured, it would not be possible to measure performance in a satisfactory manner. Organizational leaders would be dependent either on measures that had grave weaknesses or on much cruder measures such as rules of thumb and intuition.

And in nonmarket organizations, such as the defense bureaucracy, leaders are forced to adopt different methods of control over sub-units, which also has serious consequences. In an attempt to structure the situation so that the lower levels of the hierarchy will perform as desired, leadership frequently specifies detailed rules or standard operating procedures (SOPs) by which lower units are to operate. These rules, however, tend to become an end in themselves rather than a means to an end. In market organizations, with a price system acting as a set of sufficient statistics, the means of regulating behavior and the ends of the organization are congruent. In nonmarket organizations, operating without sets of sufficient statistics, the means (or the detailed rules specified by the senior leadership) tend to become independent of the ends and, in fact, tend to replace the ends. This phenomenon of "goal displacement," identified by Robert Merton[40] is a major problem in nonmarket organizations.[41]

The difficulty in measuring performance does not reduce the necessity of doing so. Measurement requires the aggregation of data.[42] In an attempt to measure output, nonmarket organizations frequently adopt simpleminded indices that can easily be quantified and therefore understood. These measures, however, frequently are not valid,[43] as we have seen.

Even though such measures have serious problems, they are widely used. In nonmarket organizations, senior leadership is continually required to justify programs, budgetary allocations, and the like. As a means of defense senior leaders will use the measures without qualification. As information flows through the organization away from "operational" areas, it tends to take on overtones of objective reality. Because senior leaders frequently do not have effective ways to challenge the information coming to them (except in the intuitive sense that "something isn't right here"), there is the distinct possibility that they will become captive to the data. Arthur Ross has noted "how public officials deceive themselves with statistics of impeccable quality."[44] Thus, although situations may not degenerate into Cyert and March's "hopeless confusion," problems of nonmeasurability of programs and difficulties in establishing quality control in nonmarket organizations may lead at the least to poor performance, modest confusion, or, at the worst, to program failure.

The nature of organizational programs can compound the dilemma of measurement. Organizational programs are designed to deal with recurring situations and to do so, organizations develop standard operating procedures. When dealing with routine situations, organizations implement problem-solving activities with which they are familiar. When confronted with nonroutine situations—which Herbert Simon calls "non-programmed"[45]—organizations still attempt to use the routine SOPs or they fall back to more generalized problem-solving activity characterized by judgment, intuition, and rule-of-thumb solutions. Either approach to a nonroutine situation is generally inadequate, inappropriate, or leads to error. However, without sufficient statistics to measure performance, the error may not be recognized until there is undeniable evidence that programs have failed—which is frequently hard to come by. Daniel Katz and Robert Kahn, in a discussion of the use of organizational SOPs in solving nonroutine situations note that "organizations often suffer from the failure to recognize the dilemma character of a situation and from blind persistence in sticking to terms of reference on the basis of which the problem is insolvable . . . [because organization] is by definition a set of restrictions for focusing attention upon certain content areas and for narrowing the cognitive style to certain types of procedures."[46]

Structural variables such as excessive hierarchy or parochialism thus present the analyst of foreign policy decision making with a fruitful vineyard to harvest explanations of failure. Organizations and their leaders are not unaware of these structural problems and have attempted to construct defenses to counteract some of the negative aspects of hierarchical organization. To mitigate problems of hierarchy, leaders can bypass conventional routes to insure that those who have information communicate it. Roger Hilsman notes that President John Kennedy used this technique on occasion.[47] However, bypassing layers of the hierarchy is time consuming (it takes a great deal of time for leaders to find out to whom they need to talk) and often results in lowered morale, as superiors who are by-passed become resentful. Other techniques for dealing with problems of hierarchy include the use of task forces, mechanisms for inspection, investigative procedures or units, outside experts, and statistical controls. Defenses against parochialism include rotation of personnel and conferences between leaders and program personnel.[48] Frequent rotation, however, causes other problems, such as the lack of in-depth knowledge about a problem among those who are supposed to be specialists. One of the various defenses against hierarchy may aggravate the problem of the blockage of information flow. Afraid that they are not receiving all the information because of "subversives" within the hierarchy, superiors emphasize loyalty as a criterion in selecting staff. Excessive demands for loyalty may reduce the flow of fresh ideas and critical views reaching the superior.[49] Thus the known defenses against structural problems, all of which are inadequate in the first place, tend to introduce or aggravate other problems in a hierarchy. Wilensky states, "All governments—totalitarian or free, parliamentary or not, with planned or less planned economies—are plagued by pathologies of hierarchy, agency rivalry, and secrecy; all generate an urgent demand for 'all of the facts' and 'short-run estimates.' . . . Defenses against structural and doctrinal roots of intelligence failures in the area of foreign policy are, therefore, universally weak and preconceptions are enduring."[50]

Organizational decision making can be viewed, then, as a process of solving immediate problems with short-range solutions by invoking standard programs and repertoires. As Lindblom, Hilsman, and others have noted, this incremental decision making results in apparently inconsistent organizational behavior as policy outputs change frequently.[51] Applications of the concepts developed by theorists of the decision analysis approach have provided greater insight into organizational decision making by closing the gap between the theoretical ideal of rational decisions and the empirical reality.[52] The decision analysis approach centers its attention on the internal characteristics of the organization such as limitations of individuals within the organization in solving problems, constraints introduced by the small group, and problems resulting from the very structure of the organizational unit. In general, outputs of the organization are seen as the result of these internal characteristics. Thus, policy output hinges on variables that earlier theorists would not normally have associated with decision making. Of even more interest is the fact that outputs of the organization that will affect the external environment are frequently made without fundamental consideration of that environment or the effect that program choices might have on it; programs are chosen simply because they resolve certain problems within the organization.

Despite the many insights into the sources of organizational decision processes, one major problem area remains for the advocates of the decision analysis approach. Most of the analysis assumes that organizations, especially in the market sector, are able to adapt and learn despite all of the constraints upon the process of decision. Consider the following propositions from Cyert and March:

1. "The firm learns from its experience."
2. The business firm is "an adaptive institution."
3. "Organizations exhibit . . . adaptive behavior over time." [53]

Firms adapt, according to Cyert and March, by changing goals, by changing rules about what to pay attention to and what to ignore (attention rules), by changing search rules, or by changing more than one of these. In short, the organization learns ("adapts") by altering its standard operating procedures in these areas.

However, considerable tension exists between the notion that despite great obstacles ("constraints") firms are able to adapt and the fact that some obstacles may be so severe that adaptive behavior is prevented. The distinction between when organizations are able to function as "adaptively rational" institutions and when constraints are severe enough to block adaptation or cripple the organization is simply not clear. Evidence that firms are not always able to adapt is readily available from examples like the collapse of the Penn Central Railroad in 1970, Ford Motor Company's experience with the Edsel, Lockheed Aircraft Corporation's problems with a series of defense contracts, and the Radio Corporation of America's disastrous experience in the computer industry.

The Political Model

Some constraints of organizations have been described by advocates of the decision analysis approach. Other obstacles have been noted by students of the bureaucratic politics approach. While the decision analysis approach suggests that firms, over time, will become adaptively rational because they must adapt or become insolvent, the political model of organizational analysis suggests that individuals, groups, or sub-units of the organization are engaged in constant interorganizational warfare and that the clash may be intense enough to cripple or destroy the organization.

Although conflict within the organization is recognized in the decision analysis approach (the satisficing of various subgroups and the notion of parochial priorities and perceptions), the political model elevates this aspect of organizational behavior to center stage. In their account of the collapse of the Penn Central, Daughen and Binzen suggest that the main reason for collapse was the conflict between the senior management officials formerly of the Pennsylvania Railroad and the senior management officials of the New York Central. The struggle was so bitter and protracted that cooperation in the new effort was lacking; each side appeared to prefer that the new company fail so that the other side could be blamed. Integration of the railroads was in fact in name only.[54]

Like the decision analysis approach, the political model attempts to describe and explain rather than to prescribe. As Mouzelis notes, the focus on the political aspect of organizational behavior "opens a new perspective in organization analysis . . . [and] constitutes one of the most significant theoretical developments in recent organization theory . . . [and is] badly needed in order to reinvigorate organization theory and reestablish the balance which, unfortunately, tips heavily on the side of conservatism and triviality."[55] Graham Allison has remarked, "The gap between academic literature and the experience of participants in government is nowhere wider than at this point."[56] While academic journals are cluttered with articles purporting to test or develop parsimonious mathematical models,[57] the political model explicitly recognizes the immense number of variables that are extant in decision making. The political approach to organization theory focuses on the fact that "men share power. Men differ about what must be done. The differences matter."[58] Thus, the conflict over these differences is resolved in a political process in which

> sometimes one group committed to a course of action triumphs over other groups fighting for other alternatives. Equally often, however, different groups pulling in different directions produce as a result, or better a resultant—a mixture of conflicting preferences and unequal power of various individuals—distinct from what any person or group intended. . . . Hundreds of issues compete for players' attention every day. Each player is forced to fix upon his issues for that day, deal with them in their own terms, and rush on to the next. Thus the character of emerging issues and the pace at which the game is played converge to yield . . . "decisions" and "actions" as collages.[59]

The conflict in most organizations is hidden from the outside observer and may not even be apparent to the observer inside the organization because "intense political activity is scrupulously and skillfully camouflaged so that the resulting policies appear to be in harmony with the official ideology and the organizational codebook."[60] To "understand" the political model, the analyst must develop a sense for the players, the games, the coalitions, the bargains, and the confusion extant in any large-scale bureaucracy.

The focus on the internal politics of organizations and their relation to the organizational output has developed haltingly; only recently have analysts begun to probe intensely into this area of organizational behavior. It is therefore less developed than decision analysis, and, even more than the other recent theories, offers primarily insights into decision making rather than empirically confirmed "laws." Its evidence derives predominantly from the observations of individuals who have engaged in decision making and the perhaps unintended accounts of bureaucratic infighting in memoirs, diaries, and other materials. Thus, "we are very far from having a conceptual framework."[61]

Melville Dalton based his pioneering book about management and organizational politics upon his lengthy experience in several firms. Dalton brings to the surface the internal political activity by which organization members pursue their own or group interests and attempt to consolidate their positions of influence and power within the organization even at the expense of more pervasive organizational interests. Dalton focuses upon the fact that a formal organization chart, with its neat and clear lines of authority and communication, conceals an informal structure composed of constantly changing cliques that cut across the organization both laterally and vertically. These cliques—which emerge, fight over issues that arise within the organization, and then disappear—are so important, according to Dalton, that the internal health or disorder of an organization can be explained by understanding the cliques and the conflicts in which they are engaged.[62] The memoirs and diaries of participants, as well as some historical accounts of specific organizations, lend substantial credence to Dalton's description of organizational infighting among various groups.[63]

A second major insight into the analysis of organizational politics and conflict was provided by Michel Crozier in his study of the French governmental bureaucracy. Rather than cliques that cut across both the vertical and the horizontal structure of the organization, Crozier found highly cohesive sub-units of the organization that were formed around work groups. These groups, existing in a highly stratified and stable bureaucracy, tended to be hostile to all other groups. Internal conflict centered around the utilization of the formal rules and regulations of the bureaucracy as a means of increasing the influence of the particular group. Since the formal rules of any organization can never take into account all problems, the areas of uncertainty provide the setting for conflict between groups.[64] Other more current anecdotal evidence indicates that the manipulation of the formal rules to enhance subgroup purposes exists in the American federal bureaucracy as well.[65]

The study of bureaucratic politics in the area of foreign policy has also just begun in earnest. Samuel Huntington's study of the politics of military strategy formulation is a pioneering work.[66] In recent years, the work of Graham Allison, Morton Halperin, I. M. Destler, Richard Neustadt, and others has provided additional evidence of the impact of bureaucratic politics on policy formulation and execution.[67]

Individuals and groups, according to these analysts, tend to pursue interests that are heavily influenced by the parochial perceptions and priorities of those individuals and groups. Such a narrow approach leads easily to the belief that the particular problems with which they are concerned are the most crucial issues facing the organization as a whole. Allison accounts for much of the American behavior during the Cuban missile crisis by delineating the interagency conflicts and the parochial priorities and perceptions of the participants.[68]

The study of organizational politics has not yet advanced to the point where analysts have clearly identified the conditions under which organizational infighting will be more or less intense. Dalton's arguments lead one to conclude that internal political activity occurs at all times over all issues, including the most trivial.[69] At the same time, it is evident that internal political activity increases when disagreement over goals exists. And it has already been established here that there is less agreement on goals in governmental organizations than in nongovernmental organizations.[70] By definition, then, internal political activity would tend to be more intense and prolonged in governmental organizations. The analyst should be surprised to discover governmental organizations in which political activity is minimal. Thus Crozier's contribution—the defending of a group's prerogatives against other groups within governmental bureaucracies—is important.[71] By combining Dalton's description of intense activity (even over trivial issues), Levy and Truman's suggestion that internal political activity is more intense in organizations where goals are subject to dispute, and Crozier's contribution that subgroups within governmental units defend the sub-unit even at the cost of "larger" goals, it may be possible to build a more useful description of behavior in governmental organizations that would clarify how and why policy is formulated, executed, and monitored.

The major weakness of the political model is related to its strength. By focusing narrowly on the conflict within the organization, one tends to lose sight of the crucial fact that much of this conflict is shaped and governed by the hierarchy of the governmental structure. Weber pointed out long ago that individuals have power in at least a rough relationship to their position in the formal hierarchy. While the individual mail carrier can, in concert with other individual carriers, undertake actions that can quickly snarl the functioning of the economy and the political system (as in a postal strike, for example), no one can deny that the carrier's ability to influence events is insignificant when compared to the potential of the staff assistant to the president. Of course, realization of the power of the individuals at the lower level of the hierarchy to disrupt the smooth functioning of the organization provides a good reason to pursue the question that is central to the political model—who influences whom and to what extent?

Yet because there is a crude relationship between formal position in the hierarchy and power, it is possible to ask whether the separation of the decision analysis approach and the political model introduces an artificial distinction. When one couples the aphorism of the political model that "where you stand depends on where you sit" with Cyert and March's idea of quasi resolution of conflict, a strong case may be made for the contention that the political model merely offers deeper insights into the process of the quasi resolution of conflict (or lack of it) in organizations and thus fits in as a submodel of decision analysis.

In addition, the political model tends to focus exclusively on intra-organizational conflict at the expense of viewing the organization in terms of its relationship to the environment. Policy and programs, according to the political model, are dependent upon the results of internal conflict and the conflict is undertaken without too much regard for the environment.

Thus the political model permits one to produce powerful explanations for events within the organization, such as the collapse of the Penn Central or the New York newspaper strikes in the 1960s. But it does not permit the analyst to produce equally cogent explanations for the effect of events external to the organization and the response of individuals and ultimately the organization to these events. After all, the members of the group that decided the course of United States action during the Cuban missile crisis were responding to changes in the environment—the Soviet introduction of a range of "offensive" weapons into Cuba.

The Open System

While the political model focuses on internal conflict, the open system model attempts to describe both the relationship of the organization to the environment and the relationship of the various units of the organization to each other. Borrowing heavily from cybernetics and systems concepts, this model views the organization as a social system composed of various subsystems. The subsystems are, in turn, complex systems linked to the larger organization by mutually interdependent bonds. The organization as a whole is linked to other organizations and the general environment.[72] Cybernetic and systems approaches emphasize the flow and content of communications within the organizations as means of holding the organization together and permitting it to function in the environment.[73] Open system theorists are not interested in the internal structure and properties of each subsystem, "but only in their interaction and its relevance to the larger system."[74]

Open system analysts argue that the organization cannot be described simply by describing the properties of the subsystems. To assume that the organization as a whole is isomorphic to the smaller units is to fall prey to the fallacy of composition.[75] Rather, each level shares characteristics of the organization as a whole, at the same time maintaining certain properties unique to that level. The various subsystems are linked together but are also semi-autonomous.

In describing and explaining organizational behavior, analysts using the open system approach focus on the flow of information within the organization and between the organization and its environment. Karl Deutsch's model of foreign policy decision making uses the flow of communications as a means of identifying several sources of distortion and error that lead to poor output. The organization monitors the output through the feedback concept; if the effect of the output is negative, either the organization changes its behavior or programs fail. It is the ability to steer, Deutsch argues, that helps prevent organizational disaster. While Deutsch identifies six major areas of failure that will cause the organization to collapse, the conditions under which each operates (or does not operate) are not specified.[76] Indeed, Deutsch raises the possibility that despite the existence of one or more of these failures, the organization may not collapse or change its output because it has enough "power" to manipulate the environment. Deutsch confronts an old dilemma when he defines power as "not to have to give in, and to force the environment or the other person to do so. Power . . . is the priority of output over intake, the ability to talk instead of listen. In a sense, it is the ability to afford not to learn."[77] Just when does an organization have enough power that it can manipulate the environment rather than making internal changes to adapt to its inadequate or inappropriate outputs?

When open system analysts talk about self-destroying systems, nonviable systems, viable systems, and self-developing systems, it is not clear whether they are discussing the internal attributes of the system or the ability of the system to manipulate the environment. We are back, then, to the questions raised when we began the discussion of modern approaches to organization theory:

> Under what conditions do organizations adapt or fail to adapt to the environment?

> If they are successful in maintaining themselves, is it because they learned from or manipulated the environment?

These questions lead to a broader question. When organizational theorists discuss the modern approaches—decision analysis, differentiating market and nonmarket organizations, political conflict, and open system—are they really differentiating several distinct approaches or are they defining one approach with different emphases?

The systems approach focuses on links between units of the organization and between the organization and the environment. This approach "black boxes" the internal characteristics of the sub-units in favor of the exchange between them. Although it is possible to describe the nature of the exchanges between the units, it is difficult to explain how or why the policy originated within the unit. The political conflict and decision analysis approaches, on the other hand, fill this void by examining the internal characteristics and activity of the units. In the political conflict approach, policy output is hinged to internal conflict—in which the actors pay only marginal attention to the external environment. Similarly, decision analysis is only marginally concerned with the impact of the environment.[78]

Each of the recent approaches appears to provide a partial explanation for organizational behavior. Yet substantial problems remain. Suppose, for example, that a governmental organization undertakes a series of programs that provoke a considerable number of the clients to invade and do serious damage to the headquarters: What caused the outburst? An inability of the organization to monitor the environment or a breakdown of communications within the organization or between the organization and its clients (open systems questions)? Poor or outdated standard programs that had become rigid and unable to deal with contemporary problems (a decision analysis question)? Internal political activity within the organization that crippled its ability to respond to the needs of its clients (a political conflict question)? Or a combination of all three types of problems?

Organized Anarchies and the "Garbage Can"

The preceding discussion of modern approaches should make it clear that no single approach to the analysis of organizational behavior is dominant. In fact, organization theory is more of a "jungle" through which the analyst must hack a path than a clear, concise body of knowledge that helps the student organize, analyze, and explain.[79] However, all of the earlier approaches share, at least to some degree, the notion that there is a relationship between what happens and the desires of people in the organizations. Whether the organization is seen as a purposive entity pursuing objectives on the basis of some function designed to minimize costs and maximize gains or as an arena for internal conflict that is influenced by the organizational structure and processes—the underlying assumption is that people *know what they are doing.*

The basic premises of the organized anarchy theory—or, as it is less reverently known, the "garbage can theory"—are the opposite. "Events happen, and if they are afterwards described in a systematic fashion as decisions, it expresses more man's ability to form post factum theories of his own behavior than his ability to make goal-oriented decisions through established structures and processes."[80] The garbage can approach is particularly appropriate "in a situation where both activation and definition of the situation are changing, where several participants are activated (in generating solutions, testing solutions, and reacting), where the definition of the situation is complex, involving many values and decision-making variables, so that the situation is difficult to analyze and it is difficult to see and compare the consequences of existing alternatives."[81]

Advocates of the organized anarchy approach first note that modern organizations are large, complex, organized systems. Within the system, members interact self-consciously with one another. Todd LaPorte has produced a working definition of organized social complexity.[82] According to LaPorte, the degree of complexity (Q) is a function of the number of components of the system (C_i), the relative differentiation (or variety) of the components (D_j), and the degree of interdependence (I_k) among the components. The greater the C_i, D_j, and I_k, the greater the

Q. Thus, organized complex systems can be measured by the formula

$$Q_x = (C_i, D_j, I_k)$$

Components may be defined as persons (or groups) in the system where (1) sufficient consensus exists about the position so that individuals (or groups) are objects of expectations and actions by other individuals (or groups) in the system and where (2) the individuals (or groups) recognize the legitimacy of the expectations of others and react either positively to those expectations or in such a way as to prevent expulsion from the complex system. Differentiation is measured by the degree of mutual exclusiveness of the activities distributed throughout the organization. Thus an organization that has numerous individuals assigned to perform similar tasks would be far less differentiated than an organization in which members perform different tasks. LaPorte suggests that it might be possible to measure the degree of differentiation through the use of formal job descriptions or through survey analysis.[83] The differentiation of the national security bureaucracy could be measured, for example, by noting the number of specialized job descriptions that existed at any given time. Then the analyst could compare the number at time t and at time $t + 1$ to determine if the bureaucracy was becoming more or less differentiated. Using this method, it could be shown that the national security bureaucracy in 1940 was far less differentiated than the bureaucracy of 1965 or 1975.

Construction of an operational definition of interdependence is a major problem. In any complex system, various kinds of resources are being exchanged—money, people, information, services, and so on. For resource R_1 (let us say "operational authority"—the ability to issue orders based on authority in the hierarchy), individual (or group) B may be dependent on A. For resource R_2 (let us say "operational information"—such as reports, evaluations, and information about an ongoing program), A may be dependent on B. For resource R_3 (let us say "budgetary allocation"—money allocated to pay for various program operations), both A and B are dependent on C. In this area of mapping interdependencies, students of organizations

130

have had difficulties because the formal aspects of organizations (such as position in the hierarchy and ability to issue orders) conceal webs of relationships that, although formally hidden from view, are of extreme importance (such as personal relationships, common interests, etc.). Skilled politicians learn these webs of interdependence by osmosis, but researchers cannot. Thus, countless descriptions of formal organizational relationships have often masked the real centers of power.[84]

If we attempt to measure organized complexity with the formula $Q_x = (C_i, D_j, I_k)r_n$, where r is the resources being exchanged, by holding D_j and I_k constant while increasing the number of C_i, it should be apparent that the organized system will tend toward disintegration because an increase in the number of components will cause the information flow between the components to increase. Increased information flow, in turn, causes pressure to build for increased differentiation and integration to counteract the tendency toward disintegration and confusion.[85]

Students of complexity, such as LaPorte, note that organizations have undergone great increases in size and differentiation while, at the same time, technological and other changes have made national security bureaucracies more interdependent. For example, the whole strategic force structure of the United States is critically dependent on the intelligence function, which is designed to provide warning time prior to an attack by an adversary. Should that intelligence system fail, much of the retaliatory force could be destroyed. Chapter three provided an outline of the command structure for Vietnam operations (figure 1, p. 41) that illustrates how extremely complex organizations have become. Students of the organized anarchy school have noted how bureaucracies have grown into "mega-organizations."

In addition to increasing size, complexity, and differentiation, several other variables are identified as being of importance in the "garbage can":

a. A variety of poorly defined and inconsistent preferences. We have already seen that there is little consensus, on other than the broadest generalities, about the real meaning of "providing for the common defense." The lack of consensus about what one should be doing has many pervasive consequences for management.

b. Processes, both organizational and technological, that are not completely understood by members of the organization. Many people who work in complex systems do not understand much of what goes on about them, either because the system or the technology is so complex that it can be understood by only a few specialists or because it has grown so large that nobody understands it. Numerous reports on the organizations of the Defense Department have confirmed the fact that no one completely understands how it operates.[86] Thus, the question arises: "Who's in charge here?" And because it appears that nearly everyone is in charge of a part, no one is in charge of it all. The organization runs, seemingly, according to rules of its own.

c. Participation by members of the organization that varies according to the issue and the time available. While this study has focused on Rolling Thunder, it should be apparent that many other problems also concerned senior policymakers, not only in the area of foreign policy (relations with Soviet Union, China, Europe, NATO, for example) but also in domestic policy (the state of the economy, domestic elections). Thus what really happens at the top of organizations may be far different from the image of calm deliberation and careful consideration of issues that incumbent policymakers would like the public to envision. In reality, senior decision makers rush from issue to issue, trying to deal with rapidly moving events over which they have little control. That many senior officials work sixteen- or eighteen-hour days seems more of a testimony to the confusion and bewildering array of issues that confront them than to orderly planning and "wise" policymaking.

d. The load on the system. The fact that policymakers are overloaded means that they can attend to only a very few issues out of the hundreds that demand attention. Many "decisions" are in fact made *by flight* (hoping the problem goes away) and by *oversight*. Many problems that should rise to the top do not. A prime example of this was the profound disagreement in 1963 between the analysts in the Department of State and those in the Department of Defense over "progress" in the war in South Vietnam, which should have been resolved in a rational system by argument at the highest level of government. Instead, the disagreement over substance turned into a disagreement over procedure, probably because senior policymakers (Rusk and McNamara) were busy with other problems that, at the time, appeared to be more important than what was happening in South Vietnam.

e. The nature of the structural channels that direct the flow of problems to choices or the flow of participants to choices. Once a hierarchy grows to a certain point, the bureaucratic maze may simply be too confusing for the rat. Despite all of the detailed routing procedures for information transmission that are developed, information gets lost or is sent to the wrong people. Or, in the crush of immediacy, the wrong people may be directed to a problem (or the right people left out). These are common problems in complex mega-organizations.

f. Ambiguity in the external environment. In the area of formulating policy or evaluating the impact of programs, seldom do analysts find "smoking guns" (undeniable evidence) that clearly indicate results. The environment is unstable and obscure. Technologies change, new coalitions form in other governments, policy debates occur within other governments and information about those debates is sketchy at best. Clear evidence of program failure or success is hard to come by since both program advocates and opponents frequently use the same evidence to argue their respective cases. For example, the environment is so ambiguous that when two analysts in the Defense Intelligence Agency predicted the forthcoming Tet offensive, their prediction was derided by others and by their superior using the same information as the analysts.[87] Similar ambiguity occurred before the Japanese struck Pearl Harbor.[88] Rolling Thunder operations were also characterized by ambiguity as a result of inadequate indicators.

g. The amount of time available for decision. Time is one of the most precious quantities in organized anarchies. The more time that is available, the more participants will become involved. Under ambiguous conditions in the external environment more and more participants with divergent views will be attracted to the problem. Participation by many seems to guar-

Rolling Thunder

antee that the decision will become the work of a committee, which frequently condenses opposing viewpoints into the lowest common denominator. In Rolling Thunder operations, more and more people joined the coalition favoring de-escalation, but only after overwhelming evidence against the program had been assembled was the policy changed.[89]

Summary

The study of organizations has progressed far from the idea of a rational, purposive organization that is efficient and effective. Modern theories of organizational behavior—decision analysis, differentiation of market and nonmarket organizations, the political model, open system approaches, and the organized anarchies approach—represent a wide range of ideas and approaches through which the student must struggle. In order to determine why it took so long for the bureaucracy to recognize that Rolling Thunder operations were not succeeding, we need to try to synthesize this theoretical morass into a coherent framework for understanding the process of decision making in national security bureaucracies. Then the process of adaptation and learning can be brought into clearer perspective. To these tasks we now turn.

6. Organizations, Foreign Policy, and Adaptation

This study began with the observation that something had gone dramatically wrong with American foreign policy toward Indochina. From 1961 to 1968, senior policymakers had designed a policy that set essentially unlimited ends (or goals) supposedly to be achieved with only limited means. It was initially hypothesized that satisfying explanations for this puzzle could be found if organizational processes and politics were examined. But the evidence in chapters one through four reveals major problems with the data collected about program performance as well as with the feedback mechanisms themselves. Therefore, the nature of the organization's exchange with the environment must first be analyzed. This is an "open system" question, for which neither the decision analysis nor the bureaucratic politics paradigm will be adequate.

The task now before us is to build a theory of decision making specific to the arena of foreign and defense policy. Analysis of the formal organizational structure is not very helpful in explaining how and why policy decisions are made, programs are developed, and programs are evaluated. The formal structure, however, is important because it provides the "setting" for policy decisions and for program implementation and evaluation. Formal position in the hierarchy equips some individuals with the means to influence policymaking, others with the means to influence program implementation, and still others with the means to influence the monitoring and evaluating of those programs. Thus the further up in the hierarchy one is, the greater chance one has of influencing policy. But if one has a greater chance to influence policy, he will probably have a lesser chance to influence program implementation. The practical impact of this irony is felt by many senior policymakers who are frustrated by the task of confronting the bureaucracy as it implements (and frequently mashes) carefully designed and delicate policy decisions. The captain of an American destroyer in the Gulf of Tonkin may have more influence in the implementation of a carefully planned policy of "signaling" North Vietnamese leaders of the American determination to defend South Vietnam than does the secretary of state or the chairman of the Joint Chiefs of Staff. The flight commander of a wing of F-105 fighter-bombers operating over Hanoi who orders his aircraft to jettison their bomb loads in order to prepare for air-to-air combat with North Vietnamese MIGs can obliterate months of sensitive diplomatic effort to begin negotiations if the bombs fall into "unauthorized" areas.

In numerous situations, then, the implementation of programs substantially affects policy. And, to carry this point a bit further, when an analyst is attempting to determine the relative power of various players, the type of issue (e.g., policymaking, program implementation, or program monitoring) is a useful indicator. In some cases, formal position in the hierarchy may mislead the analyst. For example, the individual may be well toward the top of the organization in formal terms, but if the issue under examination is a question of implementation, that formally powerful individual may in fact be powerless.

How the Formal Structure
Is Influenced by the Policy Process

These observations lead to the conclusion that formal structure of the organization is a starting point for analysis that traces the policy process. But evidence uncovered in this study suggests that the formal structure of the organization is substantially influenced by the policy process.

In the case of American operations against North Vietnam, the process of formulating policy began when the exchange between the American foreign policy apparatus and the external environment was deteriorating: the insurgency in South Vietnam was growing stronger despite massive American economic aid to South Vietnam. The manner in which the covert operations against North Vietnam were implemented was influenced by the results of an earlier disaster for the national security bureaucracy. When the Bay of Pigs failed, the Joint Chiefs of Staff, rather than the CIA, were given authority to mount covert military operations, which were implemented according to standard military procedures. These procedures, in turn, led to the Gulf of Tonkin crisis, which changed the stakes of the game by raising them to the public level.

Furthermore, during the period of covert activities, President Kennedy had created the interdepartmental task force to coordinate and supervise those operations. The formal structure of the organization was thereby changed by raising to the formal level an organization that had previously been ad hoc and that had, of course, developed informally.

Similarly, the internal struggle over strategic bombing influenced the structure of the hierarchy and the routines of the organization. The ad hoc organization that developed within the command structure for Vietnam operations for the purpose of conducting Rolling Thunder (illustrated in figure 7), with its multiple points of control and conflicting jurisdictions, was a result of internal conflict among the air force, the navy, and SAC.

These informal aspects of organization behavior are best described by the bureaucratic politics paradigm, which centers on the strife that occurs in all organizations. It is not useful to separate the bureaucratic politics paradigm from the analysis of organizational structure because the structure influences the politics, which then, in turn, influence the structure. Analysis must begin with the structure at a point in time (explaining how the structure originated) and then focus on the processes of formulation, implementation, and monitoring policy and programs. For it is in those processes that the organization itself is restructured and its output influenced.

Three Types of Bureaucratic Politics

The description of the internal politics in chapters two through four indicates that, in the hierarchy of the command structure for Vietnam operations, at least three separate forms of bureaucratic politics were operating simultaneously. Each form influenced the others, as well as the structure and operations of the hierarchy itself. For the sake of description, they will be labeled Form A, Form B, and Form C.

When participants struggled over the problem of organizational output not achieving intended goals, they were involved in attempts to formulate new policy. Form A of bureaucratic politics focuses on existing policies and involves attempts to change the policies, the intended goals, or both. And when participants struggled over the problem that the mega-organization's exchange with the environment consistently failed to achieve desired goals, they were, above all else, dealing with the problem of ambiguity. Because the effects of Rolling Thunder could not be measured in a way that all (or most) individuals within the command structure could agree upon, the issue of Rolling Thunder could never be decided on the basis of "whose estimate is correct." Rather, it was to be decided in terms of "which coalition of participants was dominant in the organization at any given time." We are thus back to the point at which this study began. Questions about the adequacy of performance are not answered in any rational way when no method of measuring performance has been agreed upon. Those questions are answered instead through internal politics—which group can get its way? And that struggle is settled by the amount of political muscle that each group commands at the moment.

Form B of bureaucratic politics is characterized by internal fighting over how existing policies are to be implemented. Within the organization, "who gets the action" is a major issue and therefore a source of intense infighting. Struggle in Form B bureaucratic politics can last for years and current policy will be caught up in the longer-range disputes. It is not possible to explain Rolling Thunder operations without placing those operations in the context of the intense and sometimes acrimonious debate between the air force and the navy over the question of strategic bombardment. Similarly, the struggle between the Joint Chiefs and the CIA for control of covert military operations also influenced OPLAN 34-A operations. Form B bureaucratic politics played a critical role in the hierarchical structure that emerged for Vietnam operations and also contributed to the blockage in recognition of the need to adapt policies. Thus Form A and Form B bureaucratic politics interact and influence each other.

The third form of internal political activity, Form C, is the internal struggle over issues that seem trivial to an outside observer but crucial to the participants, such as reserved parking places near the main entrance to the headquarters building, keys to the executive washroom, and access to privileged dining areas. Students of organizations have observed that such concerns are evident in all hierarchies, including the command structure for Vietnam operations.[1] Form C activity also influences the other forms. For example, if a participant loses a struggle for office location close to senior officials, his lack of direct access to top officials will reduce his power to influence formulation and implementation of foreign policy.

That Form B internal political activity influenced the command structure and standard operating procedures for Rolling Thunder operations and that Form A struggle over changing Rolling Thunder was influenced by the command structure compel a synthesis of the bureaucratic politics and organizational process paradigms. A new paradigm, combining the analytic power of each and reflecting their interaction, is needed.

Rolling Thunder

A General Paradigm for Foreign and Defense Decision Making

The following general paradigm is offered. The outline and much of the terminology used by Allison are preserved for the sake of clarity.[2]

I. *Basic Unit of Analysis. Foreign Policy as Output Directed at the External Environment.* Foreign policy outputs are influenced by internal politics and processes of the organizations charged with formulating and implementing them in several important ways. The output itself is the result of the fact that foreign policy is made and executed by large-scale hierarchical bureaucracies. When leaders "make" policy, they trigger sets of organizational routines. These routines are the effective range of choice (since organizations can do only what they know how to do) but this fact is not always recognized by leadership. In the covert activities against North Vietnam, for example, the routines for collecting intelligence led to the Gulf of Tonkin crisis. The effect of that crisis was further to constrict the range of options open, since once the reprisal bombing had been executed, there were not many other options left for action against North Vietnam. The structure and routines of organizations are influenced by the internal political activity that takes place as participants struggle to change or defend existing policies and interests. Thus policy at any one time is a result of the interests of a coalition within the organization that is dominant. Part of that coalition changes relatively rapidly through elections; part of it changes less rapidly since some of the participants hold permanent government positions.

II. *Organizing Concepts. Organizations and Individuals Interacting Simultaneously.* The national security bureaucracy is composed of a constellation of organizations that function according to predetermined routines. Within that constellation, individuals maintain a primary attachment to one of the organizations. When an issue emerges, key questions also arise: Who plays? (which organizations and individuals?) What determines positions or stands on an issue? How is influence determined? And how does the mesh of organizational and individual interests combine to form policy?

Organizations, Foreign Policy, and Adaptation

A. *Who Plays?* What organizations and individuals are involved and to what degree? The principal agencies and departments for foreign affairs are those defined as the national security apparatus. In Vietnam operations, part of that apparatus was involved, while part was not. In Washington, the agencies dominant in the apparatus were involved in varying degrees, depending on how many other issues demanded attention at the same time. Thus only a portion of the State Department was actively concerned with Vietnam affairs. The remaining portions of that department were concerned with the hundreds of other issues that were also important—NATO, the Middle East, etc. Once an organization or a sub-unit of it becomes involved, the individuals within that organization or sub-unit will also become involved. It is difficult for individuals who are not members of an organization or sub-unit charged with a particular problem to become involved unless they can demonstrate why they should be involved. Thus, which organizations "get the action" influences the bureaucratic politics because the organization either gives them access to the problem or denies that access.

B. *Factored Problems and Fractionated Power.* The complexity of issues in foreign policy requires that problems be divided into manageable units. The existence of a national security apparatus at time t means that any problem at time $t + 1$ will be divided among the various agencies and departments of that apparatus. In the United States, the structure of the national security bureaucracy organized to cope with the exigencies of World War II has remained fairly stable. Over time, those agencies and departments have grown and have developed now-familiar routines for dealing with problems. When a new problem arises that does not fit neatly into the apparatus at time t, then an internal struggle develops that shapes the hierarchy so that it can cope with the new problem. At time $t + 1$ a new hierarchical structure will emerge, but the distance between times t and $t + 1$ will be substantial. For example, when the oil embargo in 1973 created problems that concerned energy and national security, the existing structure was not organized to cope with them. An internal struggle broke out and only five years later was that struggle resolved (at least temporarily) by the creation of the Department of Energy.

The process of dividing known problems also provides a source of internal political activity. Internal disputes arise between players and participants over which group of players or organizations should have primary responsibility for the problem. When primary responsibility is divided among more than one organization, coordination—and the operation of the program—is likely to be poor or inadequate.

C. *The Hierarchical Form of Bureaucratic Organization.* Because of the factoring of problems, power is also fractionated among participants. But the overall organization is characterized by a hierarchy in which senior participants have the right to decide based upon their position in that hierarchy. The form of hierarchy structures the answer to "What is the game?" because it provides formal access channels and influences patterns of information flow. Hierarchy distributes players among positions and rewards them with advantages and disadvantages. In addition to the formal organization, hierarchies also include informal networks, which overlap and cut across formal lines of authority, thus making reconstruction of internal political activity difficult for the analyst. The informal networks also influence the structure of the hierarchy through their own channels of communication, which provide different modes of access to participants than the formal structure does. Recognition of the effectiveness of informal networks may lead to reorganization of the hierarchy so that the formal structure more nearly matches the informal structure or, on the other hand, if senior officials want to break up the informal structure, the reorganization may cut previous participants out. For example, after word leaked to the press in 1966 about the scheduling of air strikes against the petroleum targets, the State Department was subsequently cut out from the Rolling Thunder execute messages.

Position in the hierarchy also shapes the parochial priorities and perceptions of the participant organizations and the players. The problems that are assigned and the route of the information flow result from position in the hierarchy.

D. *Organizational Routines.* The dominant characteristic of organizational activity is its conformity to the routines or standard operating procedures (SOPS) of that organization. Organizations accomplished "their 'higher' functions, such as attending to problem areas, monitoring information, and preparing relevant responses for likely contingencies, by doing 'lower' tasks—for example, preparing budgets, producing reports, and developing hardware."[3] Programs are clusters of SOPS; repertoires are groups of programs. Any organization's repertoire is limited to sets of rehearsed programs that cannot be substantially altered in any single situation. These repertoires constitute the range of choice for implementation of foreign policy. You cannot do what you do not know how to do. And this rigidity fosters a gap between policy formulation and policy implementation for no matter what policy is desired, organizations implement according to standard routines.

E. *Organizational Goals.* The primary organizational goal is survival, usually measured in terms of dollars appropriated and personnel strength authorized. Beyond that, organizations are characterized by two other goal sets. One set is externally directed—performing assigned tasks so that the exchange between the organization and its external environment is favorable to the organization. When the exchange is not favorable (however that is measured), internal political activity occurs as participants struggle to change the output, the goals, or both. Another set of goals is internally directed. Sub-units may struggle with each other over which is to perform the externally directed task and how it is to be performed. Each sub-unit has as one of its goals the performance of activity related to its area of expertise. When tasks arise that touch on a specialty of more than one unit, internal political activity takes place. Organizational imperialism is, then, an outgrowth of organizational health—dollars budgeted and bodies assigned as organizations struggle to expand. Within any complex hierarchy, competing sub-units will struggle to obtain dominance or as much of the action as possible so that sub-unit parochial priorities and perceptions can be achieved.

F. *Uncertainty Avoidance.* Organizations prefer stable operating environments. Internally, the environment can be stabilized if sub-units' drives at imperialism are muted. One mechanism for resolution of competition is agreed-upon budget splits. Sequential attention to competing goals of sub-units is another quasi resolution to conflict, which can affect immediate policy. However, agreed-upon budget splits may leave the organization somewhat unprepared if sudden demands are made upon one of the sub-units for which funds have not been provided.

Externally, organizations attempt to manipulate the external environment so that the exchange between that environment and the organization is favorable. This ideal of a negotiated environment is seldom attained. When the exchange is not favorable or the environment is unstable, internal conflict breaks out. That conflict will tend to diminish when the exchange is again perceived as favorable or the environment is stable again. But different sub-units may not perceive that the changed policy is producing the desired results, so internal pressure always exists for further attempts at manipulation of the environment.

G. *Central Coordination and Control.* Centralization vs. decentralization is a profound issue for governmental leaders. Complex problems require factoring and thus delegation of authority. But the way in which each sub-unit functions has important consequences for the other sub-units. Thus central coordination is required. But factoring has resulted in delegation of authority downward. This issue provokes constant tension in any hierarchy, and governmental agencies undergo continual reorganization as questions of centralization and decentralization arise. Furthermore, sub-units will resist coordination if it involves surrendering part of their essence to other sub-units or to "higher" authority. The military services, for example, have successfully resisted all attempts at unification, and the result has been the complex interorganizational arrangements that characterize the Department of Defense. Resistance is a common form of internal political activity that affects the command structure and the policy output of the hierarchy.

H. *Decisions of Government Leaders.* Senior managers sit atop a national security apparatus over which they can have substantial but not complete control. The position of the president in that hierarchy gives him substantial, but not complete, power as a player. Even if a president is vitally interested in a problem and devotes enormous time to it, the organizations and players charged with the issue or the routines of the organization or its sub-units may frustrate presidential power. Covert operations in Vietnam, for example, resulted in "lock-in" when the routines of the program led to an unexpected situation. Rolling Thunder confronted the president with similar problems. The president is a super-player when he decides to become actively involved in an issue, but the other players and participants are not powerless. By engaging in tactics such as leaks to the press, distorting information as it flows through the hierarchy, executing "end runs" by "going to the Hill," and the like, other players can and do influence the game and may force the president to abandon or modify his intended goals. Thus, electing new leaders may have marginal impact on existing policies even when those new leaders may be committed to change. Some of the participants in the game who are members of the "permanent government" may influence policy in ways incongruent with the expectations and demands of the leaders. At best, in the issues area of foreign policy, the American political system is only quasi-democratic since the unelected members of the permanent government have so much influence.

III. *Dominant Inference Pattern.* Foreign policy is the result of two sets of interactions—one between the external environment and the national security apparatus, the other within the apparatus between participating organizations and players in position. The first kind of interaction triggers a form of internal bureaucratic politics related to questions of outputs and goals. The second form of interaction may not be related to questions of the organization's relationship to its external environment but does influence the nature of the goals and the output. Models that posit policy as only a response to external stimuli need to be revised. Some output may not be related to external events; some clearly is related to external stimuli. The task is to sort out how the simultaneous interactions influence the foreign policy of a nation.

Rolling Thunder

The Process of Adaptation and "Learning"

Now that existing theory has been recast, the central question of this study can be examined and more powerful explanations produced. The most striking characteristic of American foreign policy toward Indochina was the contradiction between ends and means. The Tet offensive exposed that contradiction and raised questions of organizational adaptation (or lack of it) to external environmental realities.

In chapters two through four, the nature of American operations against North Vietnam and the monitoring of those programs were described. Some tentative hypotheses were offered. In chapter 5, two major questions concerning the process of adaptation were raised:

Under what conditions do organizations adapt or fail to adapt to the environment?

If they are successful in maintaining themselves, is it because they learned from or manipulated the environment?

Using the descriptive analyses of chapters one through five and the recast theory, we can now describe the process of organizational adaptation in foreign policy bureaucracies. This description has three central aspects.

I. *Adaptation as a Result of the Failure of Externally Directed Programs.* Foreign policy outputs are directed at the external environment. American foreign policy toward Vietnam in 1961–68 was characterized by programs designed to manipulate a recalcitrant external environment by force. In the early stages of that attempt, policy remained unchanged in the face of repeated program failures. Rather than changing policy, decision makers changed programs by increasing the amount of force applied to the external environment. Only when programs that were extraordinarily costly continued to fail *and* clear evidence (in the form of the Tet offensive) was available that programs of still higher cost would also probably fail did policy change. That foreign policy organizations adapt by changing policy only after costly attempts to manipulate the external environment fail is a profoundly disturbing discovery.

II. *Organizational Sources of Resistance to Adaptation.* If the analysis of adaptation must begin with the interaction between the organization and its external environment, the explanation of why it took so long for policy to change must focus on the internal characteristics of the organizations that formulated policy, implemented programs, and monitored the effects of those programs. As ongoing programs continued to fail to achieve policy objectives, stress developed within the command structure. A "performance gap"—the difference between what the organization is doing and what it could (or should) be doing[4]—developed. The existence of such a discrepancy was recognized by some sub-units of the command structure as early as 1963; it was never recognized by other sub-units. The stress in the organization as a whole sprang from the dispute over whether a performance gap existed at all or what to do about it if it did.

That recognition occurred in some sub-units early, later in others, and never in still others highlights two problems. First, the indicators and measurement techniques used in the monitoring process to obtain feedback were inadequate. Second, a conflict of interest inevitably develops when organizations charged with program implementation are also expected to monitor and evaluate those programs.

Throughout this study the distinction between policymaking, program implementation, and program monitoring has been emphasized. In certain areas of the command structure for Vietnam operations, these functions overlapped, when individuals and organizations were involved in, for example, both policymaking and program implementation. But in most areas of the command structure, program implementation is accomplished by different individuals and sub-units from those involved in policymaking. Figure 8 illustrates in schematic form the ideal policy process.

If the policy process worked as it is supposed to work, what went wrong in foreign policy toward Vietnam? Why did it take so long to adapt to external realities?

Figure 8.
The Policy Process (Idealized)

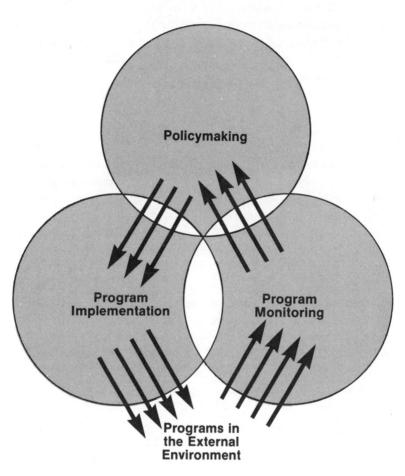

Organizations, Foreign Policy, and Adaptation

A. *The Normal Dysfunctions of Hierarchy.* Students of organizations have long pointed to the fact that the hierarchical form of bureaucratic organization produces certain efficiencies (such as specialization) but carries with it certain dysfunctions. The form of the hierarchy determines, in the main, "who plays" and "what is the game" because it provides or denies access to channels of communication and formal authority. But in a large organization with a substantial hierarchy, the right to decide on the basis of formal authority is often separated from the ability to decide on the basis of specialized skill. In addition, those who make policy at the highest levels are generally not those who implement and monitor programs. Thus a great discrepancy developed between what policymakers thought would be produced by covert activities and what was actually implemented. The same was true during Rolling Thunder. Senior participants may have the right to decide but they are not able to implement and monitor. Attempts by senior policymakers to supervise closely the actual implementation or to become involved in the collection, processing, and dissemination of intelligence are resisted by the implementing and monitoring agencies as unwarranted attempts to tell experts how to do their jobs. Although senior managers do sit atop the national security apparatus, they have only partial control.

B. *The Special Dysfunctions of Foreign Policy Hierarchies.* Foreign policy is the composite output of a plethora of organizations. The lack of agreement on all but the most general goals for national security is a peculiar handicap for foreign policy organizations. Beyond broad agreement on "the common defense" as a general goal, there are widespread disputes as to what this means in practical, day-to-day terms. Foreign policy bureaucracies are therefore characterized by intense internal political activity springing from parochial priorities and perceptions as well as from drives for sub-unit imperialism. Factored problems, fractionated power, and hierarchical structure only aggravate the internal political struggles.

The lack of agreement on goals also means that there is no agreed-upon way of measuring organizational performance. That there is no accepted method for measuring performance does not reduce the need to measure it. Thus goal displacement, in which the means to an end become the ends themselves, is a common characteristic of program implementation. The profound problem of measuring foreign policy performance has largely been neglected by political scientists.

C. *Organizational Intelligence.* Intelligence does not consist simply of knowledge about the capabilities and intentions of other states. It also involves knowledge about internal capabilities. No senior manager of a market-oriented organization would accept the argument that "sales personnel are the only capable judges of sales activity." Market organizations normally have an organizational sub-unit (usually known as the comptroller) that cross-checks performance reports. But in national security bureaucracies, the argument is widely accepted that "when it comes to fighting, the professional military are the only capable judges."[5] In practical terms, acceptance of this view has meant that, in the main, the military supervises the agencies charged with the implementation of military programs.

D. *Recognition of the Need to Adapt.* The agencies charged with monitoring military programs that are supervised by the military are structured very much like the military. Mechanistically structured organizations are less likely to recognize the need to adapt than are organically structured organizations. Furthermore, when military-supervised organizations monitor program implementation by military agencies, an inevitable conflict of interest develops. It is an old point made by students of organizations and reconfirmed in this study: valid program evaluations cannot be done by organizations charged with implementing them. In the case of the covert operations, this meant the clandestine agencies as well as the ad hoc interdepartmental task force that supervised those operations; in the case of Rolling Thunder, it meant military intelligence (i.e., air force intelligence, navy intelligence, etc.) and intelligence agencies of the Department of Defense (the Defense Intelligence Agency and the National Security Agency). Individuals in these monitoring agencies are, of course, not necessarily malevolent, but there is an inherent conflict of interest that those individuals may themselves not recognize. In some cases, however, the conflict of interest did produce deliberate distortion of feedback, which short-circuited the policy process. Some of the organizational characteristics, particularly the structure, were shaped and influenced by the internal process and politics. In contrast to the idealized schematic description of the policy process in figure 8, the actual process as it functioned with regard to operations against North Vietnam is illustrated in figure 9.

III. *The Process of Adaptation*. The need to adapt was recognized first in the few monitoring agencies not charged with the actual implementation: the Bureau of Intelligence and Research and the Board of National Estimates. The process of adaptation includes several steps: A discrepancy develops between what the organization is doing and what it could (or should) be doing. That performance gap is perceived by subunits with no vested interests in the programs that are the source of the gap. Internal stress develops as struggle breaks out within the organization as a whole. Coalitions form favoring various policy and program alternatives. Policy changes when one of the coalitions becomes dominant. The growth of that coalition is facilitated by the continuing negative exchange with the external environment. When policy changes, new programs are implemented, and those programs are monitored. Adaptation to external realities therefore involves the formation of a performance gap, its recognition, internal struggle over alternative sources of action, policy change, new program implementation, and new program monitoring.[6] At each of these stages, the "normal" dysfunctions of hierarchy in general and the "special" dysfunctions of foreign policy bureaucracy in particular may block adaptation. At each stage in the adaptive process, those obstacles must be overcome.

Summary

That Rolling Thunder operations persisted as long as they did is the fundamental puzzle of this study. The evidence uncovered here promotes several troubling conclusions. First, much of what comes out of the national security bureaucracy as foreign policy may be related more to the internal needs of the

Figure 9.
The Policy Process for Operations against North Vietnam,
1961–1968

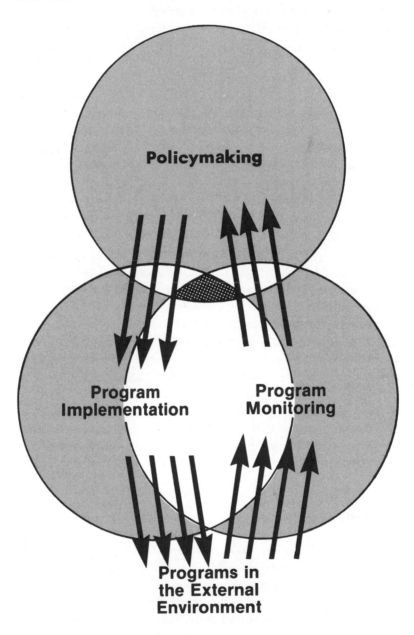

bureaucracy than to the problem at hand. The bureaucracy's internal needs may carry so much influence because the environment external to the national security bureaucracy is full of ambiguity, the mega-organization itself is so complex, differentiated, and interdependent that its members do not understand how it operates, the hundreds of issues that compete for attention result in an overloaded system, there is a lack of consensus about what should be done, and there are significant problems in measuring what is being done. These difficulties lead to the general conclusion that much of the foreign policy decision process resembles an organized anarchy. Coherent and comprehensive explanations probably reveal more about the ability to construct explanations than about the actual process. This is not to suggest that all activity within a complex system such as the national security bureaucracy would fit under the label of anarchy. Indeed, much of the day-to-day activity may be purposive and linked to objectives that are understood and shared by people within and without the bureaucracy. But the ambiguity, lack of consensus, lack of methods of measuring performance, and so on, suggest that at the "macro" end of the organization where policies are made and programs—such as Rolling Thunder—are developed, implemented, and measured, "anarchy" is a more useful descriptive term than is "coherent."

Epilogue

It would be pleasant to conclude this study by suggesting that it is possible for organizations and people in them to learn from experience. After all, most authors (and, hopefully, people who read their books) prefer happy endings. But this story does not end so neatly. When Rolling Thunder ended in 1968, the bombing of North Vietnam was not stopped. The United States resumed massive bombing of North Vietnam in December 1972. Those raids, using B-52 strategic bombers as well as regular fighter-bombers, were of even greater intensity than Rolling Thunder. The organization had not learned from the Rolling Thunder failure. The Christmas bombing of Hanoi in 1972 shocked many, but members of the Nixon administration claimed that the new raids "forced" North Vietnam to sign the peace agreements with the United States. That argument appears to be more propaganda than substance, for the agreement finally signed was basically the same agreement that was released to the press *before* the Christmas bombings began.

But a more fundamental problem about organizational learning and adaptation is suggested by the resumption of bombing: It appears that the national security bureaucracy may be unable to learn. The halt in Rolling Thunder can be seen in retrospect not as strategy but as tactical adaptation or learning. The strategic lesson—that the use of conventional bombing against a non-industrial country organized to fight and win a revolutionary war will fail—appears to be unlearn-able. Despite all the evidence accumulated during World War II, the Korean War, and finally the Vietnam War, that conventional strategic bombing plays only a marginal role in the determination of victory (actions at sea and on the ground are the critical determinants), leaders and organizations are still committed to a theory of victory through the air. Further-more, organizations are constructed in such a manner as to implement this theory. And if the theory of conventional stra-tegic air power is incorrect or only partially correct, then for what purpose is the United States maintaining massive capa-bilities in this area?

The above question is, of course, a "rational" one. But the organizations charged with these programs will resist learning if it threatens their essence. Apparently, in the case of Rolling Thunder, no learning took place, since bombing was subse-quently used in another attempt to apply force to a recalcitrant environment.

There is one final point. If the theory of victory through the air is still predominant, and organizations are maintained for achieving that end, we should expect that, during the next crisis or conflict, advocates will again try to seduce policy-makers with the will-o'-the-wisp of quick victory.

Notes

Chapter 1

1. Quoted in Dan Oberdorfer, *Tet!,* p. 105.
2. Bernard Brodie, *War and Politics,* p. 115.
3. A necessarily incomplete list of studies of American involvement in Vietnam would include Chester L. Cooper, *The Lost Crusade*; Frances FitzGerald, *Fire in the Lake*; Townsend Hoopes, *The Limits of Intervention*; Robert Shaplen, *The Lost Revolution*; and Ralph Stavins, Richard J. Barnet, and Marcus G. Raskin, *Washington Plans an Aggressive War.* For an excellent account of some of the decision making, see Robert L. Gallucci, *Neither Peace Nor Honor.*
4. This is the thrust of the argument made by David Halberstam in *The Best and the Brightest.*
5. Daniel Ellsberg concludes that "the right wing of the Republican Party tattooed on the skins of politicians and bureaucrats alike some vivid impressions of what could happen to a liberal Administration that chanced to be in office the day a red flag rose over Saigon . . . [and therefore five American presidents] chose knowingly to prolong the war, and in most cases to expand it" (Daniel Ellsberg, *Papers on the War,* pp. 101, 125).
6. Richard DuBoff, "Business Ideology and Foreign Policy," pp. 16–31.
7. Frederic Branfman, "Beyond the Pentagon Papers," pp. 294–313.

   There are three versions of the Pentagon Papers. The first, published by the *New York Times,* contains an interpretive text by reporters for the newspaper as well as some of the

documents contained in the original United States government volumes. This version will not be cited. The second,
published by Beacon Press after Senator Mike Gravel of
Alaska read part of the papers into the *Congressional Record,* contains almost all of the original text of the United
States government volumes, most of the documents, and
some documents apparently not included in the original
United States government study. This version will hereafter
be referred to as *Gravel.* The third version, published by the
Government Printing Office, contains almost all of the text
and documents except those censored prior to declassifica-
tion. Most of the material censored from the Government
Printing Office edition can be found in the Gravel version.
The Government Printing Office edition combined the 47
chapters of the original study into 12 volumes. This edition
will hereafter be referred to as *GPO.* For as complete a set
of the papers as possible, the *Gravel* and *GPO* versions must
be combined.

Finally, the *Gravel* edition combined the 47 chapters into
four volumes and then numbered the pages consecutively in
each volume. The *GPO* version simply combined the chapters into a volume without renumbering the pages. Each
GPO volume is paginated as the original chapter was paginated; therefore the citations for the *GPO* version will include the chapter number and then the page. Citations for
the *Gravel* edition will include the volume number and then
the page.

Since the *Gravel* edition contains most of the censored material from the *GPO* edition, it is possible to determine
quickly what type of material the United States government
considers sensitive enough to censor. Most of the excised material deals with American diplomatic moves and involvement in the coup d'etat that overthrew Premier Diem of
South Vietnam in November 1963. Other censored material
includes secret bombing of the Ho Chi Minh Trail in Laos in
the early 1960s and information dealing with certain intelligence activities.

8. Leslie H. Gelb, "Vietnam." Gelb also argues that the emotional,
intellectual, and professional commitments of many officials
within the national security apparatus to continued prosecution of the war also played a role in explaining why the
United States remained in Vietnam for as long as it did.
Gelb directed the task force within the Defense Department
that assembled the history of American involvement in Vietnam. The study is commonly known as the Pentagon Papers.

9. See, for example, Lyndon B. Johnson, *The Vantage Point.*

10. Irvin L. Janis, *Victims of Groupthink.* Janis is careful to state
    that not all of the eight group pressures he identifies lead
    toward what he terms foreign policy "fiascoes." Janis cites
    the decision making during the Cuban missile crisis of Octo-
    ber 1962 and the formation of the Marshall Plan following
    World War II as instances where group decision making re-
    sulted in careful examination of alternatives, potential conse-
    quences of those alternatives, and the adoption of what he
    terms sound policy. Janis cites the Vietnam policymakers as
    having a high degree of group cohesiveness. At the same
    time, he is careful to state that group decision making is
    only one of several possible variables at work and repeatedly
    reminds the reader that he is engaged in hypothesis con-
    struction rather than complete explanation.

    For an earlier attempt to apply findings from social psy-
    chology to foreign policy decision making, see Joseph
    de Rivera, *The Psychological Dimension of Foreign Policy.*
11. George Reedy, *The Twilight of the Presidency.*
12. See, for example, Morton H. Halperin, *Bureaucratic Politics and
    Foreign Policy*; Graham Allison, *Essence of Decision,* espe-
    cially chaps. 3–6.
13. Halperin, *Bureaucratic Politics,* pp. 235–60.
14. Nicholas Henry, *Public Administration and Public Affairs,*
    p. 55.
15. The national security bureaucracy, as herein defined, includes
    the White House staff charged with foreign policy and de-
    fense matters, the National Security Council, the Depart-
    ment of State, the Department of Defense, the Central Intel-
    ligence Agency, and the Agency for International
    Development. Other agencies are also involved in foreign
    policy and defense matters in specific areas such as the de-
    partments of Commerce, Agriculture, Labor, and the Trea-
    sury. However, the major functions of these agencies lie out-
    side the realm of national security policymaking. One
    central problem for the White House is to find out which
    agencies need to be involved, which agencies are involved,
    and which agency or agencies should have central authority.
16. The term "insurgent forces" as used here means those opposed
    to the existence of the government in Saigon. The terminol-
    ogy that should be used to describe these forces is the subject
    of an unresolved dispute. Until 1965 the forces opposed to
    the Saigon government were composed almost entirely of in-
    dividuals who had been in South Vietnam prior to the start
    of the insurgency in the late 1950s, at least some of whom
    arrived in South Vietnam from North Vietnam shortly after
    the Geneva Agreements were signed in 1954 ending the

French effort at halting the guerrilla movement throughout
all of Indochina. After 1965 North Vietnamese Army (NVA)
regulars began arriving in South Vietnam to fill out existing
units of the Viet Cong insurgents. In addition, regular units
of the NVA were also sent to South Vietnam after 1965. Thus
a dispute arose: was the war in South Vietnam an insurgency of individuals within South Vietnam or was it an invasion by infiltration of North Vietnamese forces? American
intelligence referred to the forces opposed to the government
in Saigon as VC/NVA forces. In order to avoid a proliferation
of abbreviations here, the VC/NVA forces will be called insurgent forces. The term is meant to include both North Vietnamese regulars infiltrated into Viet Cong units and North
Vietnamese regular army units operating in South Vietnam,
Laos, and Cambodia.

17. Janis, *Groupthink.*
18. Department of State, Bureau of Intelligence and Research,
"Statistics on the War Effort in South Vietnam Show Unfa-
vorable Trends," 22 October 1963, in *Gravel,* 2:770-80. The
protest by the Department of Defense and the Rusk apology
is noted in ibid., p. 189.
19. The muting of opposing or divergent views into one common
statement is called "waffling," which means a blurring of
viewpoint into a joint statement, carefully constructed by the
participants so that it reflects minimal consensus and,
through careful choice of language, hides disagreements.
20. *Gravel,* 2:189.
21. A second set of questions, also raised by this incident, but not
dealt with in this study, focuses on senior civilian perceptions of the famous dictum of Karl von Clausewitz that war
is a continuation of politics by other means and accordingly
"can never be separated from political intercourse, and if, in
the consideration of the matter, this occurs anywhere, all the
threads of the different relations are in a certain sense broken, and we have before us a senseless thing without an object" (Karl von Clausewitz, *On War,* p. 596). Bernard Brodie
remarked that "this understanding has never fully got across
to the great majority of those people who think and write
about war, and even less to those who fight it." As a result,
"Men have fought and bled for values held too sacred to
question and yet in fact juvenile" (Brodie, *War and Politics,*
pp. 2-3).

In this incident, Secretary Rusk seems to have misunderstood the dictum. For an extended discussion of American
attitudes toward war and politics, see Robert Osgood,

Idealism and Realism in American Foreign Policy, and Bernard Brodie, *Strategy in the Missile Age.*

22. External environment is defined simply as other organizations, cultures, natural resources, individuals, etc. See Merlin B. Brinkerhoff and Phillip R. Kunz, eds., *Complex Organizations and Their Environments,* p. xix.

23. The presence of large units of troops of the Chinese Communist People's Liberation Army in the areas of Hanoi and Haiphong in North Vietnam eliminated invasion of North Vietnam as a viable alternative. American forces would have come into contact with the Chinese forces, and the war would have expanded rapidly.

24. This definition of failure is the same as that used by Tang Tsou in *America's Failure in China, 1941-1950.* Tsou defines failure as "the imbalance between means and ends" and the concomitant "inability to use military power purposefully to achieve political objectives [or] the unwillingness and inability to abandon unattainable goals in order to avoid entanglements in a hopeless cause" (p. ix).

Chapter 2

1. President Kennedy's decision is documented in National Security Action Memorandum 52, dated 11 May 1961. The National Security Action Memorandum (NSAM) was the device by which presidents Kennedy and Johnson issued formal instructions and communicated results of high-level decisions to the national security bureaucracy. The resources for the covert activities are described in a memorandum from Brigadier General Edward G. Lansdale, an American expert on guerrilla warfare, to General Maxwell D. Taylor, President Kennedy's military adviser, "Resources for Unconventional Warfare, S.E. Asia." See *Gravel,* 2:637-49.

2. The necessity of coordination of the activities of numerous organizations in several countries was undoubtedly a major reason for the unsystematic activities. As Graham Allison noted, "Alternatives requiring coordination of several organizations . . . are likely to be poor" (*Essence of Decision,* p. 90).

3. Exactly *when* the North Vietnamese became involved and *what* caused the insurgency were the subjects of intensive investigation by the researchers who compiled the Pentagon Papers. See *GPO,* IV.A.5., "Origins of the Insurgency in South Vietnam, 1954-1960," especially the summary.

4. In the memorandum describing the existing resources for uncon-

ventional warfare, General Lansdale refers to operations throughout Southeast Asia during the 1950s, including operations in North Vietnam, but unfortunately does not describe them in detail. See "Resources for Unconventional Warfare, S.E. Asia" in *Gravel,* 2:642–49.

5. For a more detailed discussion of the idea of signaling with covert operations, see Allen S. Whiting and James Clay Thompson, "Intelligence and Bureaucratic Quicksand." For a more general discussion of the concept of signaling in the context of foreign policy decision making, see Thomas Schelling, *The Strategy of Conflict,* and Roberta Wohlstetter, *Pearl Harbor.* For a series of fascinating hypotheses about deliberate signaling of false intentions as a tactic of deception and surprise in foreign policy, see Barton Whaley, *Codeword Barbarossa.* Whaley deals with the issue of Stalin's alleged surprise by the attack on Russia by Germany in 1941.

6. *GPO,* IV.C.2.(a), "Evolution of the War: Military Pressures against North Vietnam, Action and Debate, Feb.–Jun. 1964," p. i.

7. Theodore Sorensen, *Kennedy,* p. 630.

8. *GPO,* IV.C.2.(a), "Evolution of the War: Military Pressures against North Vietnam, Action and Debate, Feb.–Jun. 1964," p. 5.

9. Ibid., p. i.

10. Ibid., p. 1.

11. Ibid., p. i.

12. In a televised address on 4 August 1964, President Johnson characterized the attacks as "open aggression on the high seas against the United States of America." In a speech the next day at Syracuse University, he stated that North Vietnam "has now struck out on the high seas in an act of aggression." Secretary of State Dean Rusk, in a nationwide televised interview on 5 August 1964, noted that the ships were in international waters "in which we have a perfect right to be" (*GPO,* V.A., "Justification of the War: Public Statements," pp. D-12, 13, 16).

13. What actually happened on the nights of 2 and 4 August has been a matter of some dispute. For a detailed account of the OPLAN 34-A actions, the movements of American destroyers, and the North Vietnamese actions, see *GPO,* IV.C.2.(b), "Evolution of the War: Military Pressures against North Vietnam, July–October 1964," pp. 1–15. See also Joseph C. Goulden, *Truth Is the First Casualty,* for an account based on interviews with many of the American crewmen, as well as on testimony before Congress. On the basis of those interviews, Goulden reports that one American ship almost

opened fire on the other during the confusion surrounding the attack. An American crewman had a target in his sights and was ordered to fire. He refused until the other destroyer could be located. The target in his sights turned out to be the other American destroyer.

Most of the other accounts of the Gulf of Tonkin crisis are based on these two primary sources. Part of the *GPO* edition dealing with the crisis was censored. The missing portion is available in *Gravel*, 5:325. The portion censored from the *GPO* edition deals primarily with the fact that the American destroyers were intercepting North Vietnamese radio communications and the electronic signals from the North Vietnamese radar sets.

14. *GPO,* IV.C.2.(a), "Evolution of the War: Military Pressures against North Vietnam, Action and Debate, Feb.–June 1964," p. 1.
15. For details on the use of Chinese Nationalist guerrillas against North Vietnam, see Allen S. Whiting, "What Nixon Must Do to Make Friends in Peking."
16. *GPO,* V.A., "Justification of the War: Public Statements," p. D-18.
17. Whiting, "What Nixon Must Do."
18. Allison, *Essence,* p. 89.
19. *GPO,* IV.C.2.(b), "Evolution of the War: Military Pressures against North Vietnam, July–October 1964," p. iii.
20. Ibid., pp. 19–21.
21. Ibid., p. iii.
22. Secretary of Defense Robert McNamara discovered this resistance during the Cuban missile crisis. During close questioning of Chief of Naval Operations Admiral George Andersen about the navy's plans on how to stop Soviet ships, Admiral Andersen waved a copy of the navy's *Manual of Navy Regulations* in McNamara's face and told him not to worry because all the procedures were detailed in that volume. For a description of this incident, see Allison, *Essence,* pp. 133–34.
23. *GPO,* IV.C.2.(b), "Evolution of the War: Military Pressures against North Vietnam, July–October 1964," pp. 27–32; *Gravel,* 3:195–96. The authorization for increased cross-border operations from South Vietnam into Laos without Laotian Premier Souvanna Phouma's knowledge was censored from the *GPO* version but is available in *Gravel.*
24. *GPO,* IV.C.3., "Evolution of the War: The Rolling Thunder Program Begins," p. iii.
25. See "Questions and Answers on Covert Activities, Sept. 1964," *Gravel,* 3:571–75.

26. *GPO,* IV.C.2.(c), "Evolution of the War: Military Pressures against North Vietnam, November–December 1964," p. i.
27. Ibid., p. 5.
28. Dan Rather and Gary Paul Gates, *The Palace Guard.*
29. In addition, by allowing George Ball to express his views, members of the group could (and did) believe that they had examined all alternatives. This false sense of being open to all views is one of the problems of group decision making noted by Irving L. Janis in *Victims of Groupthink.*
30. How the ambassador measured "South Vietnamese morale" is not clear and is not documented. On the basis of operational experience, it is possible to suggest that "morale" was "measured" by discussing programs with a few South Vietnamese leaders and military personnel who expressed their beliefs. Thus the strong convictions of the ambassador may have been based on a totally unscientific sampling. How often arguments that have such momentous consequences in terms of men's lives and fortunes are made on the basis of selected discussions! Such an argument is almost impossible to refute, since it is virtually impossible to measure "morale." The argument takes on a life of its own.
31. One of the authors of the Pentagon Papers comments that the National Security Council principals "appear to have assumed rather low motivation on the part of the DRV [North Vietnam]. Either this or they were overly optimistic regarding the threat value of U.S. military might, or both" (*GPO,* IV.C.2.(c), "Evolution of the War: Military Pressures against North Vietnam, November–December 1964," p. 52). Among the additional pressures approved in November 1964 was a slight increase in the air reconnaissance and air strike activity over Laos (Project Barrel Roll). In November and December 1964 Barrel Roll was to consist of two missions by four aircraft per week—a total of eight sorties over a territory of thousands of square miles! How eight weekly sorties were to frighten the same North Vietnamese leadership that fought a French army of 250,000 men to a standstill affirms the remarkable optimism or naivete of the National Security Council principals. In December 1964 the JCS questioned the Defense Intelligence Agency (DIA) as to why there had been no noticeable North Vietnamese or Chinese Communist response to the increase of armed reconnaissance of Barrel Roll. DIA concluded that the Communists probably did not notice that the slightly increased activity represented a significant U.S. decision to increase covert activities. Ibid., pp. 62–63.

Since specific Barrel Roll schedules had to be approved at

the level of the secretary of defense or higher (presumably the White House), one has the rather ludicrous image of extremely busy and powerful men approving miniscule air operations they thought to be a significant increase and then having the other side not notice those operations. One simple reason that the additional operations may not have been noticed is the possibility that many of the sorties may have been out of the range of North Vietnamese radar.

32. The target lists were part of Operations Plan (OPLAN) 37-64. OPLAN 37-64, then, was a series of standard instructions informing the members of the organization what was expected of them when action was triggered. *GPO,* IV.C.3., "Evolution of the War: The Rolling Thunder Program Begins," pp. 3–5.

33. Allison, *Essence,* p. 79.

34. *GPO,* IV.C.3., "Evolution of the War: The Rolling Thunder Program Begins," p. v.

35. Ibid., p. 28.

36. Ibid., p. iii. Italics in original.

37. Bundy's arguments may be found in a lengthy memorandum to the president, "A Policy of Sustained Reprisal." Taylor's arguments are in a cable to the president from Saigon. The JCS arguments for heavy bombing over an eight-week program were included in a memorandum to Secretary McNamara. Similar arguments were made by CINCPAC in a series of comments on Ambassador Taylor's cable to the president. These documents are in ibid., pp. 31–47. Rostow's argument was circulated after the Gulf of Tonkin crisis. These documents and comments on the Rostow argument by other agencies are in *GPO,* IV.C.2.(b), "Evolution of the War: Military Pressures against North Vietnam, July–October 1964," pp. 21–22, 34–37.

38. See Chairman, Joint Chiefs of Staff Memorandum 221–265, summarized in *GPO,* IV.C.3., "Evolution of the War: The Rolling Thunder Program Begins," p. xvi.

39. Allison, *Essence,* p. 178.

40. *New York Times,* 7 January 1975, p. 2.

41. This problem is of central concern to students of war such as Bernard Brodie. Brodie constantly attacks political leadership for permitting "events" to get out of hand. In reality, when "events" get out of hand, it may be that leadership has lost control of its own organizations. For Brodie's castigation of political leadership, see *Strategy in the Missile Age* and *War and Politics.* For an even broader historical and sometimes humorous perspective, see Charles Fair, *From the Jaws of Victory.*

42. The popular analogy at that time was "two scorpions in a bottle."

43. President Kennedy stated that the United States was engaged in what he termed a "twilight war." This type of conflict "is another type of war, new in its intensity, ancient in its origin—war by guerrillas, subversives, insurgents, assassins, war by ambush instead of combat, by infiltration instead of aggression, seeking victory by eroding and exhausting the enemy instead of engaging him. . . . It requires a whole new strategy, a wholly different kind of military training" (quoted in Roger Hilsman, *To Move a Nation,* p. 410).

44. This is a bald summary of the debate about American strategy that was conducted in the late 1950s and early 1960s. For some of the relevant literature, see Maxwell D. Taylor, *The Uncertain Trumpet*; Herman Kahn, *On Thermonuclear War*; William W. Kaufman, *The McNamara Strategy*; and Brodie, *Strategy.*

45. President Kennedy directed the national security bureaucracy to attach strong importance "to the programs designed to counter Communist indirect aggression, which I regard as a grave threat during the 1960s." See National Security Action Memorandum 132, 19 February 1962, in *Gravel,* 2:666.

46. A classic statement of the domino theory is in the Joint Chiefs of Staff Memorandum 33-62, 13 January 1962, in *Gravel,* 2:797–98.

47. For a list of 16 critical beliefs that were widely held by senior decision makers in the post–World War II period, see Morton H. Halperin, *Bureaucratic Politics and Foreign Policy,* pp. 11–12.

48. From a normative perspective, it might be useful to have *more* parochial priorities at this level of discussion. Questioning of the fundamental assumption that South Vietnam was critical to American security would have been useful in the early 1960s before the major buildup of American forces occurred.

49. The agencies involved were the departments of Defense and State, the CIA, the United States Information Agency, the International Cooperation Administration, and the Office of the President. The implementing document is National Security Action Memorandum 52, 11 May 1961. See *Gravel,* 2:637–43.

50. Allison, *Essence,* p. 93.

51. For evidence of the buildup of pressure for continued or expanded action, see the cable from the U.S. Embassy, Saigon, to the State Department, 13 October 1961, and General Maxwell Taylor's report to the president, 3 November 1961, in *Gravel,* 2:651–54. In Washington, the Joint Chiefs argued, without supporting documents, that the operations under

OPLAN 34-A were effective and should continue. See Joint
Chiefs of Staff Memorandum 426-64, 19 May 1964, in
Gravel, 3:511–12.
52. Allison, *Essence,* p. 91.

Chapter 3

1. See *GPO,* IV.C.3., "The Rolling Thunder Program Begins: January–June, 1965," pp. 1–149; ibid., IV.C.7., "The Air War in North
   Vietnam"; and ibid., IV.C.10., "Statistical Survey of the War,
   North and South: 1965–1967," p. 21.
2. Department of Defense, *Dictionary of U.S. Military Terms,* pp.
   203–4.
3. Ibid., p. 211.
4. Jack Broughton, *Thud Ridge,* p. 23. Broughton was a pilot engaged in Rolling Thunder operations.
5. The pilots flying fighter aircraft referred to B-52s as BUF's. "BUF
   stands for big ugly fellows in polite circles. . . . This terminology irritated the big load drivers, and the general in
   charge of their operation issued an edict that the B-52 'Strato-
   fortress' was not to be referred to as a BUF. His edict re-
   ceived amazingly little attention outside the strategic empire" (ibid., p. 32).
6. The restrictions along the Chinese border prohibited aircraft
   from flying within a certain number of miles of that border,
   a rule that was designed to reduce the probability of U.S. aircraft flying into Chinese airspace and engaging in a dogfight
   with Chinese air defense forces. Nevertheless, a few such in-
   cidents did occur. The Hanoi and Haiphong areas were off
   limits, primarily to prevent accidental destruction of foreign
   embassies and consulates.
7. Raphael Littauer and Norman Uphoff, eds., *The Air War in Indochina,* p. 39.
8. Ibid., p. 43.
9. *GPO,* IV.C.3., "Evolution of the War: The Rolling Thunder Program Begins," p. 135.
10. Ibid.
11. Ibid.
12. Ibid., p. 138.
13. The threat to collapse may be a more common situation in
    great power–dependent power relations than has commonly
    been thought. That threat may give the small power lever-
    age in dealing with the larger power. I am indebted to Wil-
    liam Zimmerman for this phrase as a description of dyadic

relations in some circumstances. See William Zimmerman, "The Soviet Union."

14. *GPO,* IV.C.7.(a), "The Air War in North Vietnam."
15. Ibid., pp. 6–7. Ball argued that by becoming involved in Vietnam we were losing our sense of priorities.
16. Ibid., p. 8.
17. Ibid.
18. Ibid., pp. 56–57.
19. Ibid., pp. 64–65.
20. Ibid., pp. 66–67.
21. Interview with Allen S. Whiting, former director of the Far East Division of the Bureau of Intelligence and Research, 25 January 1971.
22. *GPO,* IV.C.7.(a), "The Air War in North Vietnam," p. 68.
23. Ibid., p. 72.
24. Ibid., p. 73.
25. Ibid.
26. Ibid.
27. The February Special National Intelligence Estimate is in ibid., p. 76. The March CIA study was censored from the *GPO* edition and may be found in *Gravel,* 4:71–73.
28. *GPO,* IV.C.7.(a), "The Air War in North Vietnam," pp. 88–90.
29. Ibid., pp. 110–11.
30. The effect of the Senate Foreign Relations Committee hearings is noted in ibid., pp. 116–18.
31. Ibid., pp. 136–37.
32. Ibid., pp. 142–43.
33. The bulk of the study may be found in ibid., pp. 150–60.
34. Ibid., p. 138.
35. Ibid., p. 144.
36. Ibid., pp. 166–74.
37. See David Halberstam, *The Best and the Brightest,* pp. 215–50, for an account of McNamara's ability to argue in internal meetings.
38. This internal split should give pause to analysts who posit the CIA as a monolithic organization. The evidence here suggests that CIA, like any large-scale organization, was fraught with internal disputes and contradictory views.
39. *GPO,* IV.C.7.(a), "The Air War in North Vietnam," p. 180.
40. *GPO,* IV.C.7.(b), "The Air War in North Vietnam," p. 2.
41. Ibid., pp. 4–5.
42. Ibid., p. 7.
43. Ibid., p. 22.
44. Ibid., pp. 24–42.
45. Ibid., pp. 54–58.
46. Ibid., p. 72.

47. Ibid., p. 74.

48. Ibid.

49. Ibid., p. 91.

50. Morton H. Halperin, *Bureaucratic Politics and Foreign Policy,* pp. 256–57.

51. McNamara did not take the defeat by the Stennis subcommittee without fighting back. He reassembled most of the members of the 1966 study group. Their conclusions were even more direct and bluntly critical of Rolling Thunder than they had been during the previous summer. But the internal fighting was overtaken by events.

52. *GPO,* IV.C.7.(b), "The Air War in North Vietnam," vol. II, p. 144.

53. For the study of the president's change in views, see Townsend Hoopes, *The Limits of Intervention.* See also *GPO,* IV.C.7.(b), "The Air War in North Vietnam," vol. II, pp. 141–204; and Herbert Schandler, *The Unmaking of a President.*

54. On 19 March 1968, JCS proposed attacking targets in downtown Hanoi and Haiphong that had previously been restricted. See *GPO,* IV.C.7.(b), "The Air War in North Vietnam," p. 193.

55. Graham Allison, *Essence of Decision,* p. 95.

56. *GPO,* IV.C.7.(b), "The Air War in North Vietnam," p. 114. By December 1968, the total tonnage of bombs dropped on North and South Vietnam surpassed the total dropped by U.S. forces in the European theater in World War II. About half of those were dropped on North Vietnam, more than the amount dropped during the Korean War or in the Pacific theater in World War II.

57. Littauer and Uphoff, *Air War,* p. 36.

58. Bernard Brodie, *Strategy in the Missile Age,* chap. 1.

59. Littauer and Uphoff, *Air War,* p. 1.

60. The industrial sector produced only 12 percent of the North Vietnamese GNP of $1.6 billion in 1965. When industrial installations were first targeted in 1965, JCS listed only eight facilities of major importance. *GPO,* IV.C.7.(a), "The Air War in North Vietnam," pp. 54–55.

61. Ibid., pp. 55–56.

62. For a discussion of Operation Strangle, see Robert F. Futrell, *The United States Air Force in Korea, 1950–1953.*

63. Walter F. Guzzardi, Jr., "Management of the War," p. 135.

64. Ibid.

65. Halperin, *Bureaucratic Politics,* p. 28.

66. During intelligence briefings in Washington in which both services were participating, air force officers would make disparaging remarks about performance of the navy, and the navy officers would reply in kind.

67. See Broughton, *Thud Ridge,* for those examples.
68. Thus Allison's Models II and III are in reality one model. Each emphasizes different aspects of behavior, but each also distorts behavior for the sake of emphasis.
69. David M. Shoup, "The New American Militarism," p. 55.
70. Broughton, *Thud Ridge,* p. 73.
71. Robert K. Merton, "Bureaucratic Structure and Personality."

Chapter 4

1. The external environment is herein defined as other organizations, culture, or other factors external to the organization that are taken into consideration in the decision-making behavior of individuals within the organization. See Gerald Zaltman, Robert Duncan, and Jonny Holbek, *Innovations and Organizations,* p. 114; Merlin B. Brinkerhoff and Philip R. Kunz, eds., *Complex Organizations and Their Environments,* p. xix. Defining where the organization ends and the external environment begins has been a substantial problem for organization theorists. The "boundary problem" is illustrated nicely by the dilemma facing administrators of American universities: are students members of the organization or are they its clients? For discussions of the boundary problem, see William Dill, "Environment as an Influence on Managerial Autonomy"; R. E. Emery and E. Trist, "The Causal Texture of Organizational Environments"; and D. S. Pugh, D. J. Hickson, C. R. Hinings, and C. Turner, "Dimensions of Organizational Structure."
2. Zaltman, Duncan, and Holbek, *Innovations,* p. 106.
3. Alain Enthoven and K. Wayne Smith, *How Much Is Enough?*
4. Frank Levy and Edwin Truman, "Toward A Rational Theory of Decentralization."
5. Roland N. McKean, "Criteria of Efficiency in Government Expenditures," p. 516.
6. Memorandum from Secretary of Defense Robert McNamara to the President, 30 June 1965. *GPO,* IV.C.3., "Evolution of the War: The Rolling Thunder Program Begins," p. 136. Italics are McNamara's.
7. Statement by Barry Zorthian, U.S. Embassy, Saigon. Quoted in Walter F. Guzzardi, Jr., "Management of the War," p. 236.
8. For some details of the nightmare confronting analysts, see Morris J. Blachman, "The Stupidity of Intelligence."
9. For evidence of deliberate falsification, see Sam Adams, "Vietnam Cover-Up."
10. *GPO,* IV.C.6., "U.S. Ground Strategy and Force Deployments:

1965–1967," contains evidence of a dispute between the CIA and MACV over the size of the insurgent forces. Under the MACV analysis, the insurgents would not have been able to conduct the Tet offensive.

11. *GPO,* IV.B.4., "Justification of the War: Internal Documents, The Kennedy Administration," vol. I, p. 413.
12. Jack Broughton, *Thud Ridge,* p. 23.
13. Raphael Littauer and Norman Uphoff, eds., *The Air War in Indochina,* p. 38.
14. Ibid., p. 39.
15. Ibid.
16. *Air War against North Vietnam.* Hearings before the Preparedness Investigating Subcommittee (Chairman: Sen. J. Stennis) of the Committee on Armed Services, U.S. Senate, 90th Congress, 1st Session, August 1967, p. 30.
17. Broughton, *Thud Ridge,* p. 76.
18. Ibid.
19. Blachman, "Stupidity of Intelligence."
20. The problem was a source of disputes between the services engaged in Rolling Thunder and intelligence agencies monitoring the effects on North Vietnam (CIA, DIA, and NSA). For example, a pilot would be credited with a "MIG kill" on the basis of pilot reports, but subsequent intelligence would indicate that the MIG in question had merely dived into a cloud to avoid combat. To accelerate rapidly, the MIG pilot would start his afterburner. A cloud of smoke would be emitted from the engine of the MIG, and the plane would appear to be damaged when the aircraft dove into the cloud. Intelligence would report that the MIG was not destroyed. The services would claim that the Soviets or Chinese were supplying additional MIGs to make up the losses. Thus more Soviet or Chinese aid was posited than may have been shipped. This, in turn, may have created the impression that the Soviets or Chinese had more "leverage" with the North Vietnamese than they really did.
21. Victor Thompson, *Modern Organizations,* p. 6.
22. Donald Schon, *Technology and Change.*
23. Thompson, *Modern Organizations,* pp. 152–77.
24. Robert Presthus, *The Organizational Society,* p. 33.
25. Harold Wilensky, *Organizational Intelligence,* p. 43.
26. Michel Crozier, *The Bureaucratic Phenomenon.*
27. Tom Burns and G. M. Stalker, *The Management of Innovation.*
28. Peter Karsten et al., "ROTC, My Lai, and the Volunteer Army."
29. Burns and Stalker, *Innovation.*
30. Ibid; see also Chris Argyris, *Integrating the Individual and the Organization.*

31. Guzzardi, "Management," p. 135.
32. W. V. Haney, "Serial Communication of Information in Organizations."
33. Ibid., p. 160.
34. Levy and Truman, "Rational Theory of Decentralization."
35. Herbert A. Simon, *The Shape of Automation for Men and Management*, p. 18.
36. *GPO*, IV.C.7.(a), p. 180.
37. Blachman, "Stupidity of Intelligence."
38. Statement by Barry Zorthian, U.S. Embassy, Saigon. Quoted in Guzzardi, "Management," p. 236.

Chapter 5

1. Karl Weick, *The Social Psychology of Organizing*, p. 18.
2. James March, ed., *Handbook of Organizations*, p. 5.
3. When analysts organize information, they apply a framework or theoretical structure as an organizing device in order to make sense of a mass of data. At the core of descriptive analysis is the critical notion that the personal values of the analyst are excised from the description of what exists or has existed. For example, Herman Kahn notes that while individuals are aware of the horror of cancer, most of them would prefer that the illustrations in a book on surgery would not be captioned "A particularly deplorable tumor," or "Good health is preferable to this kind of cancer." Most people would prefer that the surgeon have a good description that is reasonably value free. Herman Kahn, *Thinking about the Unthinkable*, p. 26.

Closely related to description is prediction. The accuracy of a prediction is directly related to the richness of the description and explanation of the relationships of the variables involved. Unfortunately, the lack of rich description and explanation has not prevented many analysts from making predictions. Predictions, of course, are frequently colored by the normative values of the analyst. Normative values also affect description unless care is taken to remain as "value free" as possible. The prediction of an individual emotionally committed to an outcome must be carefully evaluated. Simply because a strong supporter of a political candidate states that the candidate will win does not mean that the candidate will in fact win the election. Finally, prescriptive analysis centers around what the analyst feels "ought to be." Prescriptions are based upon the normative values. These values may be those of the analyst or may be offered on the basis of the values of another individual ("if you want X, here is what you must do"). For a more extended discussion of these types of analysis as applied to world politics, see William D. Coplin, *Introduction to International Politics,* pp. 2–7. See also Irving M. Copi, *Introduction to Logic*; and Abraham Kaplan, *The Conduct of Inquiry.*

4. For example, Frederic Branfman argues that American policy in Vietnam was a result of a kind of pathology of power that inflicted American leaders. His argument is rooted in two broad normative assumptions: power corrupts men and men corrupted make immoral or amoral decisions. Neither of these assumptions has been proved even in the most rudimentary sense. Branfman, "Beyond the Pentagon Papers," pp. 294–313. For a critique of the revisionist school from different grounds, see Robert James Maddox, *The New Left and the Origins of the Cold War.*

5. Karl Marx's views on bureaucracy may be found in Robert Merton, Ailsa P. Gray, Barbara Hockey, and Hanan Selvin, eds., *Reader in Bureaucracy.* Marx's prediction about the withering away of the bureaucracy in a socialist state has clearly proven to be erroneous. Bureaucracy and complex organization are characteristics of all industrial societies without regard to ideological orientation. See Ferrel Heady, *Public Administration.*

6. Weber's description of the characteristics of bureaucracies is found in Merton, *Reader in Bureaucracy.* See also Reinhard Bendix, *Max Weber.*

7. Richard H. Hall, "The Concept of Bureaucracy"; D. S. Pugh et al., "Dimensions of Organizational Structure."

8. James G. March and Herbert A. Simon, *Organizations,* pp. 34–37.

9. Frank Gilbreth, *Primer of Scientific Management*; Frederick W. Taylor, *The Principles of Scientific Management.*

10. Taylor, *Scientific Management,* pp. 41–48, 58–64.

11. See, for example, Rensis Likert, *New Patterns in Management.*

12. Robert Kahn and Daniel Katz, "Leadership in Relation to Productivity and Morale."

13. For examples of the classical administrative approach, see Luther Gulick, "Notes on a Theory of Organization"; James Mooney, *The Principles of Organization*; John Pfiffner and Robert Presthus, *Public Administration.*

14. Herbert A. Simon, "The Proverbs of Administration." Simon argued that the "principles" offered were not in fact principles but rather were proverbs. The principles were either inconsistent with each other (how do you specialize while preserving the unity of command?) or too general to be of much use

(the idea of specialization does not distinguish between types of specialization—by place or by function). Simon's central argument is that each of the principles conceals the true complexities of a large organization and that before analysts prescribe, they should develop an adequate description.

15. Nicos Mouzelis, *Organisation and Bureaucracy,* p. 201n.

16. Lawrence Mohr argues, "Organizational behavior is Hardy-esque; it depends upon the fortuitous, complex, and obscure confluence of many distantly related streams; it depends upon solutions that happen to be there when the problems arise. There is utility in developing models for the explanation of behavior at this level, if only to drive home the point that so much of organizational behavior is not clearly goal-directed." In an attempt to develop an operational definition of the organizational goal concept, Mohr then states, "Specifically, organizational goals will be viewed as multiple rather than unitary, empirical rather than imputed, and as dichotomized into outwardly—and inwardly—oriented categories" (Lawrence B. Mohr, "The Concept of Organizational Goal," p. 472).

17. There are several possible conditions, both internal and external, under which it might be useful to view some organizations as if they were in fact unitary actors. When the following internal conditions exist, unitary models might be useful: simple tasks that require very little specialization (e.g., operations in which all that is required for task accomplishment is Taylor's "intelligent gorilla"); a highly centralized organization operating with highly authoritarian and coercive methods that may force an unusual degree of compliance with higher-level desires (Stalin's use of terror and unpredictable violence is one example); a highly automatic or computerized organization with preprogrammed operations not easily receptive to program change (the retaliatory systems employed by the Strategic Air Command is one example, and the mobilization of the German armed forces at the onset of World War I is striking as a precomputer analogous situation); extremely stable or routinized tasks involving detailed standard operating procedures not requiring frequent change (operations on an assembly line); highly decomposed organizations in which sub-units are not dependent on each other and thus may operate without regard to the organization as a whole; and a small, tightly knit organization in which members share intensely held values, thus reducing problems of parochialism, control, and communication difficulties (a conspiratorial political party along Leninist lines, perhaps). When the following external conditions exist, the

unitary model might also be useful: since external crises tend, at least in the short run, to unify organizations when dominant, widely shared values are threatened, under intense conditions of crisis, interorganizational politics might be subsumed as members rally to the defense of the organization; and a stable environment in which conditions are recurrent and predictable may lead to increased development of internal standard programs for organizational performance. These conditions, however, illustrate the aphorism that the exception proves the rule. That is, conditions of the sort suggested above are rare. In addition, some anecdotal evidence suggests that even these attributes may not make the unitary model more acceptable. For example, interorganizational politics may increase during a crisis such as bankruptcy in which members try to place the blame for failure on each other. Thus, if it is possible to find examples supporting one of the conditions listed, it is also possible to find examples in which the above conditions apparently did not influence internal politics toward a more unitary organization. I am indebted to an unpublished paper by Richard Vidmer for the discussion of the utility of the unitary actor model. See Richard F. Vidmer, "The Unitary Actor Model."

18. Simon, "Proverbs," p. 62.
19. J. David Singer and Paul Ray have identified characteristics of a rational decision as: (a) identification of the stimuli, (b) classification of the stimuli for both credibility and salience, (c) assignment of those stimuli to a general class of stimuli, (d) construction of a "definition of the situation" that needs a response, (e) a decision as to whether more information needs to be collected about both the situation and the possible responses with particular attention to the costs of further information gathering, (f) identification of alternative responses, (g) estimation of all possible outcomes of each response, (h) assignment of preference ratings for each outcome, (i) assignment of probabilities to each possible outcome, (j) combining utilities and probabilities according to consistent rules thus producing a hierarchy of preferences, and (k) selection of the optimum alternative. See J. David Singer and Paul Ray, "Decision Making in Conflict," p. 53.
20. See Herbert A. Simon, *Models of Man*; *Administrative Behavior*; *The Shape of Automation for Men and Management*; and *The Sciences of the Artificial*.
21. March and Simon, *Organizations*.
22. Richard Cyert and James March, *A Behavioral Theory of the Firm*.

23. Muzafer Sherif, *The Psychology of Social Norms*; Solomon Asch, *Social Psychology.*
24. Robert T. Golembiewski, *The Small Group; An Analysis of Social Norms,* p. 24.
25. Burleigh B. Gardner, "The Factory as a Social System."
26. Irving L. Janis, *Victims of Groupthink.*
27. In what Robert Zajonc has called "one of the most disturbing discoveries of social psychology, Solomon Asch found conclusive evidence that adult human subjects imitated a judgment that they knew was contrary to the facts, contrary to what they perceived, or both." Asch's experiments required subjects to compare the length of one line on a blackboard with three other lines, one of which was the same length as the original line. Alone, subjects averaged 93 percent accuracy in determining which two lines were of equal length. Then several confederates of Asch were introduced into the room and asked to make their judgments before the subject made his. The confederates would unanimously agree on an incorrect pair. Correct response rates dropped to 67 percent among subjects, indicating the pressure the group can exert on individuals. Patrick Suppes and M. Schlag-Rey found that conformity increased as the difficulty of required judgment increased. Janet Coleman and others found that the tendency toward stereotyped views increased in small groups as the difficulty of judgments increased. Roger Hilsman reported that State Department officials had a tendency to stereotype their views: "One official . . . said that except for their linguistic ability, the foreign-born were a detriment (because) they lacked good old Anglo-Saxon objectivity." Stanley Schacter conducted an experiment in which a view deviating from the group was forcefully argued and noted that the group decided not to invite the holder of the deviating view to the next meeting. For Zajonc's reporting of Asch's findings, see Robert Zajonc, *Social Psychology,* p. 37. Pressures toward conformity as the difficulty of judgment increased were reported in Patrick Suppes and M. Schlag-Rey, "Analysis of Social Conformity in Terms of Generalized Conditioning Models." See also Janet Coleman, R. R. Blake, and Jane Mouton, "Task Difficulty and Conformity Pressures." State Department stereotyped views are reported in Roger Hilsman, *Strategic Intelligence and National Decision,* p. 105. Ole Holsti also reports on pressures toward conformity rising as the difficulty of judgment and tension increase in Ole R. Holsti, "Individual Differences in 'Definition of the Situation.'"

28. Singer and Ray, "Decision Making in Conflict," p. 307. See also Karl Deutsch, *The Nerves of Government.*
29. Harold Wilensky, *Organizational Intelligence,* p. 45.
30. W. V. Haney, "Serial Communication of Information in Organizations."
31. Robert Presthus, *The Organizational Society,* p. 33.
32. Wilensky, *Organizational Intelligence,* pp. 47–49; Graham Allison, *Essence of Decision,* p. 81.
33. Wilensky, *Organizational Intelligence,* p. 58.
34. Roland N. McKean, "Criteria of Efficiency in Government Expenditures," pp. 516–21.
35. The constant reorganization of governmental bureaucracies presents students of public policy with a most difficult and baffling research problem—tracing the organizational structure over a period of time. During the four years that I spent in the National Security Agency, the office to which I was assigned was reorganized twice. During each reorganization, substantial changes were made in the operational responsibility of the office and its sub-units. Numerous reorganizations were also carried out in other offices of the agency. One of the results of these reorganizations was confusion on the part of agency members as to their exact operational responsibilities. Jurisdictional disputes would then flare up between sub-units. When confronted with the seemingly endless discussions over operational authority, I attempted to measure (informally) the amount of energy devoted to these jurisdictional disputes by the staff members assigned to senior officials. I estimated that at least 25 percent of the effort of these staff members was consumed by infighting over operational authority. Other observers with operational experience in the Defense Department have informally indicated that the amount of time devoted to such disputes is probably greater as one moves higher in the hierarchy.
36. Herbert A. Simon, George Kozmetsk, Harold Guetzkow, and Gordon Tyndall, "Management Uses of Figures," p. 15.
37. Frank Levy and Edwin Truman, "Toward a Rational Theory of Decentralization," p. 177. Levy and Truman are critical of attempts to consider market and nonmarket organizations as similar with respect to problems of centralization and decentralization.
38. Cyert and March, *Behavioral Theory of the Firm,* p. 82.
39. McKean, "Criteria of Efficiency," p. 516.
40. Robert K. Merton, "Bureaucratic Structure and Personality."
41. Levy and Truman note that the problem of goal displacement operates in public school systems. No matter how much lee-

way the board of education gives a school principal in hiring subordinates, the principal knows the implicit standards of the school board. Even though he may desire to innovate, if he knows that the board will regard the innovation as unorthodox, he will realize that his career may be blocked and thus will refrain from using his "unlimited" authority and choose instead to follow the implicit standard of the board. Levy and Truman, "Rational Theory of Decentralization," p. 177.

42. John P. Crecine and Ronald Brunner, *Implications of Changes in Information Processing and Communications Technology for the Governing Function.*

43. Thus the U.S. Army used "body count" as a measure of "progress" in the war in South Vietnam, while the U.S. Air Force and U.S. Navy used the number of sorties flown and tons of bombs dropped on North Vietnam. See chap. 5 for a more detailed discussion on the problems of insufficient measures.

44. Arthur Ross, "The Data Game," p. 64.

45. Herbert Simon, *Automation.*

46. Daniel Katz and Robert Kahn, *The Social Psychology of Organizations,* p. 277.

47. Roger Hilsman, *To Move a Nation.*

48. Wilensky, *Organizational Intelligence,* p. 62.

49. This is George Reedy's view of the current state of the American presidency. George Reedy, *Twilight of the Presidency.*

50. Wilensky, *Organizational Intelligence,* p. 128.

51. Charles E. Lindblom, "The Science of Muddling Through"; Hilsman, *Nation,* chap. 1.

52. See John P. Crecine, "A Computer Simulation Model of Municipal Budgeting"; and Aaron Wildavsky, *The Politics of the Budgetary Process.*

53. Cyert and March, *Behavioral Theory of the Firm,* pp. 100, 123.

54. Joseph Daughen and Peter Binzen, *The Wreck of the Penn Central.*

55. Mouzelis, *Organisation and Bureaucracy,* pp. 158–62.

56. Allison, *Essence,* p. 146.

57. Usually without examining the assumptions underlying these models. Riker's theory of coalition behavior is a case in point. The model assumes zero-sum situations and perfect information conditions—assumptions that are never met in the intense world of political conflict. Although the model may be useful for heuristic or other purposes, to treat it as a useful explanation of actual political behavior is certainly not very useful in developing explanations. The assumptions underlying the model lead to serious questions about its explanatory power. William Riker, *A Theory of Coalitions.*

58. Allison, *Essence,* p. 145.
59. Ibid.
60. Mouzelis, *Organisation and Bureaucracy,* p. 159.
61. Ibid., p. 158.
62. Melville Dalton, *Men Who Manage.*
63. In a study of the German ss—an organization that had political terror as its ruling credo and thus might fit the ideal for a "unitary" organization—Heinz Hohne found,

> The ss was never a monolithic organization; of all the manifestations of the Third Reich, the ss was the most random and the most self-contradictory. There was hardly an informer who was not at loggerheads with another of his ilk, hardly a practical political problem upon which any two senior ss leaders thought alike. . . .
>
> The ss secret files show the internal conflict only too clearly. Himmler for instance, accused ss-Gruppenfuhrer Reeder of sabotaging the ss policy of Germanization in Belgium. . . . Ohlendorf ridiculed Himmler's "blood and soil" fantasies; the RHSA (Reich Security Department) and the WVHA (ss Economic and Administrative Department) quarreled over whether Jews should be kept as slave labor or murdered; the Gestapo shot down Soviet deserters whom the SD wished to use as a Russian counter-revolutionary army. . . .
>
> In fact the ss world was a bizarre nonsensical affair, devoid of all logic. The theories hitherto advanced to explain the ss phenomenon have been equally bizarre, though superficially logical. In fact, history shows that the ss was anything but an organization constructed and directed on some diabolically efficient system; it was a product of accident and automatism. [Heinz Hohne, *The Order of the Death's Head,* pp. 12-13]

For an account of contradictory, inconsistent, and bizarre behavior by Soviet secret police, see Aleksandr I. Solzhenitsyn, *The Gulag Archipelago, 1918-1956.*
64. Michel Crozier, *The Bureaucratic Phenomenon.*
65. For an account of the use of formal rules for attaining subgroup goals, see Charles Markham, "A Democratic Vassal in King Richard's Civil Service." Fragmentary evidence that has emerged from the various Watergate investigations indicates that the Internal Revenue Service (IRS) resisted attempts by White House staff members to use IRS data for political purposes by citing formal and legal rules prohibiting such activity by IRS officials.
66. Samuel Huntington, *The Common Defense.*
67. Allison, *Essence*; Morton H. Halperin, *Bureaucratic Politics and*

Foreign Policy; I. M. Destler, *Presidents, Bureaucrats, and Foreign Policy*; Richard Neustadt, *Alliance Politics*; Morton Halperin and Arnold Kanter, eds., *Readings in American Foreign Policy*.

68. Allison, *Essence,* chaps. 5–6.
69. Dalton, *Men Who Manage.*
70. Levy and Truman, "Rational Theory of Decentralization."
71. Crozier, *Bureaucratic Phenomenon.*
72. Katz and Kahn, *Social Psychology of Organizations.*
73. Karl Deutsch, *The Nerves of Government.*
74. Mouzelis, *Organisation and Bureaucracy,* p. 149.
75. Heinz Eulau, *Micro-Macro Political Analysis,* p. 5.
76. The six failures or pathologies are the loss of power (or the loss of resources over the environment); the loss of intake (or the decline in the effectiveness of channels of information from the outside world); the loss of steering (or the loss of control over behavior of the organization or the ability to modify such behavior precisely and rapidly); the loss of depth in memory (or either the loss of the overall storage capacity of memory facilities or the decline in the effectiveness of recall, combination, screening, identification, and search criteria); the loss of capacity for partial rearrangement of the inner structure (or the decline of the process for learning limited new behavior patterns); and the loss of capacity for comprehensive or fundamental rearrangement (or the decline of the process for making comprehensive changes). Deutsch, *Nerves of Government,* pp. 221–22.
77. Ibid., p. 111.
78. John P. Crecine's study of municipal budgeting in Detroit following the civil disorders in 1966 suggests that disasters such as riots have only a marginal impact on the allocation process. In a study of the budgeting process of the Department of Defense, John P. Crecine and Gregory D. Fisher suggest that the allocation process is best understood by viewing it in terms of standardized procedures. See Crecine, "Municipal Budgeting" and John P. Crecine and Gregory D. Fisher, *On Resource Allocation in the U.S. Department of Defense.*
79. I am indebted to Professor Richard F. Vidmer of the University of Virginia for the term "jungle." Vidmer's work deals with Soviet administrative science, and he uses the term to describe the plethora of competing approaches in the Soviet Union. The term can also be used to describe the welter of American perspectives.
80. James March and Johann P. Olsen, *Ambiguity and Choice in Organizations,* p. 83.
81. Ibid., p. 85.

82. Todd R. LaPorte, "Organized Social Complexity." The discussion that follows is drawn from this important essay.
83. Ibid., p. 7.
84. See, for example, Robert Caro, *The Power Broker.* Caro's study describes how the real power to shape and influence much of the destiny of New York City lay not in the hands of the elected officials such as the mayor but in the hands of a powerful bureaucrat, Robert Moses. Moses built a web of interdependencies with other centers of political and economic power in New York in such a way that key decision-making authority was removed from the hands of elected officials and transferred to himself.
85. LaPorte, "Organized Social Complexity," p. 7.
86. See, for example, the report of the "Murphy Commission." Commission on the Organization of the Government for the Conduct of Foreign Policy.
87. McGarvey, "Intelligence."
88. Roberta Wohlstetter, *Pearl Harbor.*
89. The preceding discussion was drawn from March and Olsen, *Ambiguity and Choice.*

Chapter 6

1. Melville Dalton, *Men Who Manage*; David Halberstam, *The Best and the Brightest.* A more recent example of the importance of the struggle for office space near senior officials in order to have a greater influence on policy decisions was revealed following the resignation of President Richard M. Nixon. In the first year of the Nixon administration, Daniel P. Moynihan and Arthur M. Burns were appointed presidential assistants with responsibilities for domestic affairs. Burns chose a well-appointed, spacious office in the Executive Office Building across the street from the White House. Moynihan chose a small, cramped office in the West Wing of the White House near the president's chief of staff, H. R. Haldeman. When asked why he chose the small, cramped office in the West Wing rather than the more spacious suite across the street in the Executive Office Building, Moynihan replied, "Why, it meant I could piss standing next to Haldeman in the same toilet!" (quoted in Theodore H. White, *Breach of Faith,* p. 114).
2. Graham Allison, *Essence of Decision,* chaps. 3 and 5.
3. Ibid., p. 83.
4. Anthony Downs, *Inside Bureaucracy,* p. 191.
5. I am indebted to a conversation with David Fisher, C.P.A., for

focusing on the contrast between market and nonmarket organizations. The argument that "only the military should judge the military" would be like saying "only doctors should judge hospitals" or "only the police should judge the police."

6. This definition of adaptation is closely related to the definition of innovation by some students of innovation. Innovation, however, involves change in terms of adopting something perceived to be new by the potential unit of adoption. Adaptation as used here may involve an innovation but may also involve returning to the status quo or altering existing programs in previously known manners. All innovations involve adaptation but not all adaptations involve innovations. See Gerald Zaltman, Robert Duncan, and Jonny Holbek, *Innovations and Organizations,* pp. 7–50 for a lengthy discussion of innovation and innovation types.

Talcott Parsons has used the term "adaptation" in his analysis of basic functional requirements that all systems need in order to continue to survive. Adaptation refers to the system and its relations with the environment in obtaining necessary resources for achievement of the goals of the system. Adaptation as used here includes this aspect of organizational operation, but it is broadened here to include changing organizational goals. See Talcott Parsons, *Structure and Process in Modern Societies.*

Selected
Bibliography

Books

Allison, Graham. *Essence of Decision.* Boston: Little, Brown, 1971.
Argyris, Chris. *Integrating the Individual and the Organization.*
    New York: Wiley, 1964.
Asch, Solomon. *Social Psychology.* New York: Prentice-Hall, 1951.
Bendix, Reinhard. *Max Weber: An Intellectual Portrait.* Garden
    City, N.Y.: Doubleday, 1962.
Blachman, Morris J. "The Stupidity of Intelligence." In *Inside the*
    System, edited by Charles Peters and Timothy J. Adams,
    pp. 271–79. New York: Praeger, 1970.
Branfman, Frederic. "Beyond the Pentagon Papers: The Pathology
    of Power." In *The Senator Gravel Edition: The Pentagon Pa-*
    pers, edited by Noam Chomsky and Howard Zinn, 5:294–313.
    Boston: Beacon, 1972.
Brinkerhoff, Merlin B., and Kunz, Phillip R., eds. *Complex Organi-*
    zations and Their Environments. Dubuque, Iowa: W. C.
    Brown, 1972.
Brodie, Bernard. *Strategy in the Missile Age.* Princeton, N.J.:
    Princeton University Press, 1969.
————. *War and Politics.* New York: Macmillan, 1973.
Broughton, Jack. *Thud Ridge.* Philadelphia: Lippincott, 1969.
Burns, Tom, and Stalker, G. M. *The Management of Innovation.*
    London: Tavistock, 1961.
Caro, Robert. *The Power Broker.* New York: Knopf, 1974.
Chomsky, Noam, and Zinn, Howard. *The Senator Gravel Edition:*
    The Pentagon Papers, vol. 5. Boston: Beacon, 1972.

Selected Bibliography

Clausewitz, Karl von. *On War*. Translated from the German by O. J. Malthjis Jolles. New York: Modern Library, 1943.

Cooper, Chester L. *The Lost Crusade*. New York: Dodd, Mead, 1970.

Copi, Irving M. *Introduction to Logic*. New York: Macmillan, 1968.

Coplin, William D. *Introduction to International Politics*. Chicago: Markham, 1971.

Crozier, Michel. *The Bureaucratic Phenomenon*. Chicago: University of Chicago Press, 1964.

Cyert, Richard, and March, James. *A Behavioral Theory of the Firm*. Englewood Cliffs, N.J.: Prentice-Hall, 1963.

Dalton, Melville. *Men Who Manage*. New York: Wiley, 1959.

Daughen, Joseph, and Binzen, Peter. *The Wreck of the Penn Central*. Boston: Little, Brown, 1971.

de Rivera, Joseph. *The Psychological Dimension of Foreign Policy*. Columbus, O.: C. E. Merrill, 1968.

Destler, I. M. *Presidents, Bureaucrats, and Foreign Policy*. Princeton, N.J.: Princeton University Press, 1972.

Deutsch, Karl. *The Nerves of Government*. New York: Free Press, 1966.

Downs, Anthony. *Inside Bureaucracy*. Boston: Little, Brown, 1967.

DuBoff, Richard. "Business Ideology and Foreign Policy: The National Security Council and Vietnam." In *The Senator Gravel Edition: The Pentagon Papers*, edited by Noam Chomsky and Howard Zinn, 5:16–31, Boston: Beacon, 1972.

Ellsberg, Daniel. *Papers on the War*. New York: Simon and Schuster, 1972.

Enthoven, Alain, and Smith, K. Wayne. *How Much Is Enough? Shaping the Defense Program, 1961–1969*. New York: Harper, 1971.

Eulau, Heinz. *Micro-Macro Political Analysis: Accents on Inquiry*. Chicago: Aldine, 1969.

Fair, Charles. *From the Jaws of Victory*. New York: Norton, 1972.

FitzGerald, Frances. *Fire in the Lake*. Boston: Little, Brown, 1972.

Futrell, Robert F. *The United States Air Force in Korea, 1950–1953*. New York: Duell, Sloan, and Pearce, 1961.

Galluci, Robert L. *Neither Peace Nor Honor*. Baltimore: Johns Hopkins University Press, 1975.

Gardner, Burleigh B. "The Factory as a Social System." In *Industry and Society*, edited by W. F. Whyte, pp. 1–52. New York: McGraw-Hill, 1946.

Gilbreth, Frank. *Primer of Scientific Management*. New York: D. Van Nostrand, 1914.

Golembiewski, Robert T. *The Small Group: An Analysis of Social Norms*. Chicago: University of Chicago Press, 1962.

Goulden, Joseph C. *Truth Is the First Casualty.* Chicago: Rand McNally, 1969.

Gulick, Luther. "Notes on a Theory of Organization." In *Papers on the Science of Administration,* edited by Luther Gulick and Lyndall Urwick, pp. 1–46. New York: Columbia University Press, 1937.

Halberstam, David. *The Best and the Brightest.* New York: Random House, 1972.

Halperin, Morton H. *Bureaucratic Politics and Foreign Policy.* Washington, D.C.: Brookings Institution, 1974.

_____, and Kanter, Arnold, eds. *Readings in American Foreign Policy.* Boston: Little, Brown, 1973.

Haney, W. V. "Serial Communication of Information in Organizations." In *Concepts and Issues in Administrative Behavior,* edited by E. S. Mailick and E. H. Van Ness, pp. 154–65. Englewood Cliffs, N.J.: Prentice-Hall, 1962.

Heady, Ferrel. *Public Administration: A Comparative Approach.* Englewood Cliffs, N.J.: Prentice-Hall, 1966.

Henry, Nicholas. *Public Administration and Public Policy.* Englewood Cliffs, N.J.: Prentice-Hall, 1975.

Hilsman, Roger. *Strategic Intelligence and National Decision.* Glencoe, Ill.: Free Press, 1965.

_____. *To Move a Nation.* Garden City, N.Y.: Doubleday, 1968.

Hohne, Heinz. *The Order of the Death's Head.* Translated from the German by Richard Barry. New York: Coward-McCann, 1972.

Hoopes, Townsend. *The Limits of Intervention.* New York: David McKay, 1970.

Huntington, Samuel. *The Common Defense.* New York: Columbia University Press, 1961.

Janis, Irving L. *Victims of Groupthink.* Boston: Houghton Mifflin, 1972.

Johnson, Lyndon B. *The Vantage Point: Perspectives of the Presidency.* New York: Holt, Rinehart, and Winston, 1971.

Kahn, Herman. *On Thermonuclear War.* Princeton, N.J.: Princeton University Press, 1961.

_____. *Thinking about the Unthinkable.* New York: Horizon Press, 1972.

Kahn, Robert, and Katz, Daniel. "Leadership in Relation to Productivity and Morale." In *People and Productivity,* edited by Robert Sutermeister, pp. 131–45. New York: McGraw-Hill, 1969.

Kaplan, Abraham. *The Conduct of Inquiry.* San Francisco: Chandler, 1964.

Karsten, Peter; Berger, Ed; Flatley, Larry; Frisch, John; Gottlieb,

Selected Bibliography

Mayda; Haisley, Judy; Pexton, Larry; and Worrest, William. "ROTC, My Lai, and the Volunteer Army." In *American Defense Policy*, edited by Richard G. Head and Ervin Rokke, pp. 569–81. 3rd ed. Baltimore: Johns Hopkins University Press, 1973.

Katz, Daniel, and Kahn, Robert. *The Social Psychology of Organizations*. New York: Wiley, 1966.

Kaufman, William W. *The McNamara Strategy*. New York: Harper and Row, 1965.

LaPorte, Todd R. "Organized Social Complexity: Explication of a Concept." In *Organized Social Complexity*, edited by Todd R. LaPorte, pp. 3–39. Princeton, N.J.: Princeton University Press, 1975.

Likert, Rensis. *New Patterns in Management*. New York: McGraw-Hill, 1961.

Littauer, Raphael, and Uphoff, Norman, eds. *The Air War in Indochina*. Boston: Beacon, 1972.

McKean, Roland N. "Criteria of Efficiency in Government Expenditures." In *Public Budgeting and Finance*, edited by Robert T. Golembiewski, pp. 516–21. Itasca, Ill.: F. E. Peacock, 1968.

Maddox, Robert James. *The New Left and the Origins of the Cold War*. Princeton, N.J.: Princeton University Press, 1973.

March, James, ed. *Handbook of Organizations*. Chicago: Rand McNally, 1965.

———, and Olsen, Johann P. *Ambiguity and Choice in Organizations*. Bergen, Norway: Universitatforlaget, 1976.

———, and Simon, Herbert A. *Organizations*. New York: Wiley, 1958.

Merton, Robert K. "Bureaucratic Structure and Personality." In *Reader in Bureaucracy*, edited by Robert K. Merton, Ailsa P. Gray, Barbara Hockey, and Hanon Selvin, pp. 361–71. Glencoe, Ill.: Free Press, 1952.

Mooney, James. *The Principles of Organization*. New York: Harper and Brothers, 1939.

Mouzelis, Nicos. *Organisation and Bureaucracy*. Chicago: Aldine, 1967.

Neustadt, Richard. *Alliance Politics*. New York: Columbia University Press, 1970.

Oberdorfer, Dan. *Tet!* Garden City, N.Y.: Doubleday, 1971.

Osgood, Robert. *Idealism and Realism in American Foreign Policy*. Chicago: University of Chicago Press, 1953.

Parsons, Talcott. *Structure and Process in Modern Societies*. Glencoe, Ill.: Free Press, 1960.

Pelz, Donald, and Andrews, Frank M. *Scientists in Organizations: Productive Climates for Research and Development*. New York: Wiley, 1966.

Pfiffner, John, and Presthus, Robert. *Public Administration.* New York: Ronald Press, 1967.

Presthus, Robert. *The Organizational Society.* New York: Vintage, 1962.

Rather, Dan, and Gates, Gary Paul. *The Palace Guard.* New York: Harper and Row, 1974.

Reedy, George. *The Twilight of the Presidency.* New York: World, 1970.

Riker, William. *A Theory of Coalitions.* New Haven: Yale University Press, 1962.

Rourke, Francis. *Bureaucracy, Politics, and Public Policy.* Boston: Little, Brown, 1969.

Schandler, Herbert. *The Unmaking of a President.* Princeton, N.J.: Princeton University Press, 1977.

Schelling, Thomas. *The Strategy of Conflict.* Cambridge, Mass.: Harvard University Press, 1960.

Schon, Donald. *Technology and Change.* New York: Delacorte, 1967.

Shaplen, Robert. *The Lost Revolution.* New York: Harper and Row, 1965.

Sherif, Muzafer. *The Psychology of Social Norms.* New York: Harper and Brothers, 1936.

Simon, Herbert A. *Administrative Behavior.* New York: Macmillan, 1961.

——. *Models of Man.* New York: Wiley, 1957.

——. *The Sciences of the Artificial.* Cambridge, Mass.: MIT Press, 1969.

——. *The Shape of Automation for Men and Management.* New York: Harper and Row, 1965.

——; Kozmetsk, George; Guetzkow, Harold; and Tyndall, Gordon. "Management Uses of Figures." In *Public Budgeting and Finance,* edited by Robert T. Golembiewski, pp. 15–23. Itasca, Ill.: F. E. Peacock, 1968.

Solzhenitsyn, Aleksandr I. *The Gulag Archipelago, 1918–1956.* New York: Harper and Row, 1974.

Sorensen, Theodore. *Kennedy.* New York: Harper and Row, 1965.

Stavins, Ralph; Barnet, Richard J.; and Raskin, Marcus G. *Washington Plans an Aggressive War.* New York: Vintage, 1971.

Suppes, Patrick, and Schlag-Rey, M. "Analysis of Social Conformity in Terms of Generalized Conditioning Models." In *Mathematical Models in Small Group Processes,* edited by Joan Criswell, Herbert Solomon, and Patrick Suppes, pp. 56–94. Palo Alto, Calif.: Stanford University Press, 1962.

Taylor, Frederick W. *The Principles of Scientific Management.* New York: Harper and Brothers, 1911.

Selected Bibliography

Taylor, Maxwell D. *The Uncertain Trumpet*. New York: Harper, 1959.

Thompson, James D. *Organizations in Action*. New York: McGraw-Hill, 1967.

Thompson, Victor. *Modern Organizations*. New York: Knopf, 1961.

Tsou, Tang. *America's Failure in China, 1941–1950*. Chicago: University of Chicago Press, 1963.

Weber, Max. "The Essentials of Bureaucratic Organization." In *Reader in Bureaucracy,* edited by Robert K. Merton, Ailsa P. Gray, Barbara Hockey, and Hanon Selvin, pp. 18–26. Glencoe, Ill.: Free Press, 1952.

Weick, Karl. *The Social Psychology of Organizing*. Reading, Mass.: Addison-Wesley, 1969.

Whaley, Barton. *Codeword Barbarossa*. Cambridge, Mass.: MIT Press, 1973.

White, Theodore H. *Breach of Faith: The Fall of Richard Nixon*. New York: Atheneum/Reader's Digest, 1975.

Wildavsky, Aaron. *The Politics of the Budgetary Process*. Boston: Little, Brown, 1964.

Wilensky, Harold. *Organizational Intelligence*. New York: Basic Books, 1967.

Wohlstetter, Roberta. *Pearl Harbor: Warning and Decision*. Palo Alto, Calif.: Stanford University Press, 1962.

Zajonc, Robert. *Social Psychology: An Experimental Approach*. Belmont, Calif.: Wadsworth, 1966.

Zaltman, Gerald; Duncan, Robert; and Holbek, Jonny. *Innovations and Organizations*. New York: Wiley, 1973.

Zimmerman, William. "The Soviet Union." In *Conflict in World Politics,* edited by Steven Spiegel and Kenneth N. Waltz, pp. 38–53. Cambridge, Mass.: Winthrop, 1971.

Articles

Adams, Sam. "Vietnam Cover-Up: Playing War with Numbers." *Harper's,* May 1975, pp. 41–44.

Coleman, Janet; Blake, R. R.; and Mouton, Jane. "Task Difficulty and Conformity Pressures." *Journal of Abnormal and Social Psychology* 52 (April 1958): 120–22.

Crecine, John P. "A Computer Simulation Model of Municipal Budgeting." *Management Science* 13 (July 1967): 786–815.

Dill, William. "Environment as an Influence on Managerial Autonomy." *Administrative Science Quarterly* 2 (1958): 407–43.

Emery, R. E., and Trist, E. "The Causal Texture of Organizational Environments." *Human Relations* 18 (1965): 21–31.

Selected Bibliography

Gelb, Leslie H. "Vietnam: The System Worked." *Foreign Policy* 1 (Summer 1971): 110–73.

Guzzardi, Walter F., Jr. "Management of the War: A Tale of Two Capitals." *Fortune,* April 1967, pp. 131–41.

Hall, Richard H. "The Concept of Bureaucracy: An Empirical Assessment." *American Journal of Sociology* 68 (July 1963): 32–40.

Holsti, Ole R. "Individual Differences in 'Definition of the Situation.'" *Journal of Conflict Resolution* 13 (1970): 303–11.

Krasner, Stephen D. "Are Bureaucracies Important (Or Allison Wonderland)." *Foreign Policy* 7 (Summer 1972): 159–79.

Levy, Frank, and Truman, Edwin. "Toward a Rational Theory of Decentralization: Another View." *American Political Science Review* 65 (June 1971): 172–77.

Lindblom, Charles E. "The Science of Muddling Through." *Public Administration Review* 19 (Spring 1959): 79–88.

Markham, Charles. "A Democratic Vassal in King Richard's Civil Service." *Washington Monthly* 4 (July/August 1973): 48–56.

McGarvey, Patrick J. "DIA: Intelligence to Please." *Washington Monthly* 2 (July 1970): 68–75.

Mohr, Lawrence B. "The Concept of Organizational Goal." *American Political Science Review* 67 (June 1973): 470–81.

Pugh, D. S.; Hickson, D. J.; Hinings, C. R.; and Turner, C. "Dimensions of Organizational Structure." *Administrative Science Quarterly* 13 (June 1968): 65–105.

Ross, Arthur. "The Data Game." *Washington Monthly* 1 (February 1969): 62–71.

Shoup, David M. "The New American Militarism." *Atlantic Monthly,* April 1969, pp. 51–56.

Simon, Herbert A. "The Proverbs of Administration." *Public Administration Review* 6 (Winter 1946): 53–67.

Singer, J. David, and Ray, Paul. "Decision Making in Conflict." *Bulletin of the Menninger Clinic* 29 (September 1966): 46–59.

Whiting, Allen S. "What Nixon Must Do to Make Friends in Peking." *New York Review of Books,* 7 October 1971, pp. 27–31.

United States Government Publications

U.S., Commission on the Organization of the Government for the Conduct of Foreign Policy. *Commission on the Organization of the Government for the Conduct of Foreign Policy,* June, 1975. Summary and vols. 1–7. Washington, D.C.: Government Printing Office, 1975.

Selected Bibliography

U.S., Congress, Senate, Committee on Armed Services, *Air War against North Vietnam*. Hearings before the Preparedness Investigating Subcommittee, 90th Cong., 1st sess., 1967.
U.S., Department of Defense. *United States–GVN Relations*. 12 vols. Washington, D.C.: Government Printing Office, 1972.

United States Government Documents

U.S., Department of Defense. *The Senator Gravel Edition: The Pentagon Papers*. 4 vols. Boston: Beacon, 1972.
U.S., Department of Defense. *Dictionary of U.S. Military Terms*. New York: Praeger, 1963.

Published Reports

Crecine, John P., and Fisher, Gregory D. *On Resource Allocation in the U.S. Department of Defense*. Ann Arbor, Mich.: Institute for Public Policy Studies, 1971.
———, and Brunner, Ronald. *Implications of Changes in Information Processing and Communications Technology for the Governing Function*. Ann Arbor, Mich.: Institute for Public Policy Studies, 1971.

Newspapers

New York Times, 20 January 1961–30 April 1975.

Unpublished Materials

Vidmer, Richard F. "The Unitary Actor Model: Assumptions, Conditions, Limitations." Typewritten. Ann Arbor, Michigan, 1972.
Whiting, Allen S., and Thompson, James Clay. "Intelligence and Bureaucratic Quicksand: The U.S. in Vietnam." Mimeographed. Ann Arbor, Michigan, 1972.

Index

Index

also Organization theory: bureaucratic politics approach to
Bureaupathic behavior, 95, 96, 97
Burma, 20
Burns, Tom, 96–97

C

Carver, George, 53
China, Nationalist, 14, 19–20, 22
China, People's Republic of, 20, 23, 40–42, 164 (n. 31); possible involvement of in Vietnam War, 11, 19, 29, 51, 72; army of, 19, 161 (n. 23); as source of supplies for North Vietnam, 46–47, 50, 93, 171 (n. 20)
CIA (Central Intelligence Agency), 24; and covert operations, 16, 137, 139, 166 (n. 49); and debate over Rolling Thunder, 43, 49–55. *See also* Board of National Estimates
CINCPAC (Commander in Chief, Pacific): and covert operations, 16, 22; and initiation and escalation of Rolling Thunder, 20–21, 23, 24, 27, 42, 51, 53, 54, 71, 165 (n. 37); and Flaming Dart reprisal missions, 23, 27, 28; in command structure for Vietnam, 38, 40, 74; and Arc Light, 40
Clausewitz, Karl von, 160 (n. 21)
Combat Air Patrol ("MiG CAP"), 38
Command structure for Vietnam operations. *See* National security bureaucracy
Covert operations: hidden cost of, 14, 15, 21, 22, 140, 145; expansion of, 14, 16, 33; implementation of, 14, 21, 32–33, 137, 149, 150–51; effect of upon

North Vietnam, 15, 16, 27, 29; CIA-JCS rivalry for control of, 16, 139; use of "third-country personnel" in, 19–20; motives behind, 26, 30–31; U.S. public deceived about, 34; SOPs in, 137, 140, 145. *See also* OPLAN 34-A
Crozier, Michel, 96, 123, 124–25
Cuban missile crisis, 23, 31, 111, 124, 126, 159 (n. 10)
"Cutting Our Losses in South Vietnam," 46
Cybernetics, 126
Cyert, Richard, 110, 115, 117–18, 120, 125

D

Dalton, Melville, 123, 124
Da Nang, 40, 76
Daughen, Joseph, 121
Decision making: effect of bureaucratic politics upon, 5, 6–7; in foreign and defense policy, 5–6, 135–45, 159 (n. 10); misperceptions and shared perceptions in, 28–30, 31; and hierarchy, 95, 111–14, 135–37, 142, 149; effects of parochialism upon, 110–11, 121; problems of in non-market organizations, 116–34 passim; idealized version of, 175 (n. 19). *See also* Organization theory: decision analysis approach to; Policy formulation
Defense, Department of: conflict with the Department of State, 9–10, 132–33; and initiation of Rolling Thunder, 25; and authorization of Rolling Thunder strikes, 38; organizational structure of, 108, 132, 144; parochialism and infighting in,

Index

Index

strategic bombing applied to, 72–73, 77–80; pattern of air activities over, 76–77, 91–92; formulation of U.S. policy toward, 137, 140; and peace agreement with U.S., 155; tonnage of bombs dropped on, 169 (n. 56)

NSA (National Security Agency of the Department of Defense), 49–50, 53, 150, 177 (n. 35)

NSC (National Security Council), 24–25, 46, 164 (n. 31)

O

Operation Strangle, 73

OPLAN (Operations Plan) 34-A, 16–20, 21, 22–23, 139

OPLAN (Operations Plan) 37–64, 165 (n. 32)

Organization theory: application of to foreign policy and national security bureaucracy, 6, 93–99; origins of in work of Marx and Weber, 93, 105–6; underdevelopment and weaknesses of, 105–6, 129; scientific management school of, 106, 109; human relations school of, 107, 109; classical administrative school of, 107–9, 112; recent trends in, 109; decision analysis approach to, 109–14, 119–20, 121, 122, 125, 128; distinction between market and non-market organizations in, 115–21; bureaucratic politics approach to, 121–26, 128, 137; open system approach to, 126–28; organized anarchy or "garbage can" approach to, 129–34; unitary models in, 174–75 (n. 17)

P

Paris Peace Conference, 35, 43

Parochialism: and covert operations, 26, 32; effect of upon decision making, 110–11, 121; and specialization, 112, 113, 144; means of overcoming problems of, 118, 119; and bureaucratic politics, 124–25, 143; within hierarchies, 142, 143, 149

Pearl Harbor, 133

Penn Central Railroad, 120, 121, 126

Pentagon Papers, 50–51, 157–58 (n. 7)

Philippines, 14

Pleiku, 28

Policy formulation: role of leaders and bureaucracy in, 6–7; and program implementation, 22–23, 136, 143, 147, 149; effect of bureaucratic politics upon, 80, 124, 138, 139; in command structure for Vietnam, 137, 138, 147, 149. See also Decision making

Policy Planning Council, 25

POL (petroleum, oil, and lubricants) strikes, 42, 47–51, 52, 53, 142

Preparedness Subcommittee (United States Senate), 56

Presidency, 4, 5, 144–45, 157 (n. 5), 166 (n. 49)

Presthus, Robert, 95

Processes, organizational, 4–6, 36, 93–99, 132, 136–38, 140. See also SOPs

Program implementation: role of leaders and bureaucracy in, 6–7; effect of organizational structure upon, 15, 135–37; effect of parochialism upon, 32; effect of bureaucratic politics upon, 77–80, 138–39; and